THE HOMOEOPATHIC TREATMENT OF SMALL ANIMALS

Principles & Practice

THE HOMOEOPATHIC TREATMENT OF SMALL ANIMALS

Principles & Practice

by Christopher Day,
MA VetMB VetFFHom MRCVS

Index Compiled by
Francesca Garwood-Gowers
and Christopher Day

SAFFRON WALDEN
THE C.W. DANIEL COMPANY LIMITED

Published in Great Britain by
THE C. W. DANIEL COMPANY LIMITED
1 Church Path, Saffron Walden,
Essex CB10 1JP.

ISBN 0 85207 216 3

Reprinted 1990
Revised and updated 1992
Reprinted 1996

This book has been printed on part recycled paper

Production in association with
Book Production Consultants PLC,
25–27 High Street, Chesterton, Cambridge CB4 1ND.
Printed and bound by St Edmundsbury Press,
Bury St Edmunds, Suffolk

Dedication

To Shelagh, my wife. Her love, encouragement and untiring help have been so valuable.

'. . . . . *In spite of this my pride does not prevent me from confessing that veterinary surgeons . . . . have more skill in the treatments of old wounds than the most learned professors and members of the academics.'*

HAHNEMANN 1784

'Peruvian (Cinchona) bark, which is used as a remedy for intermittent fever, acts because it can produce symptoms similar to those of intermittent fever in healthy people.'

HAHNEMANN 1790

Acknowledgements

This book is the result of a great deal of inspiration and education received from many directions. Firstly, my parents, who are both vets, have given me so much clinical guidance down the years. My mother, too has helped me to study homoeopathy. Much of her work in this field has inspired me to use the method myself and my uncle Bernhard, a homoeopathic doctor in Germany, has been a source of inspiration to me from an early age. The courses at the Faculty of Homoeopathy have been invaluable.

I would also like to thank Jørgen and Kirsten for their philosophical stimulation, Anthony for his helpful criticism, Trevor for his advice and encouragement, Christine, Sylvia and Thérèse and their animals for help in photography and, for her stoical efforts with the manuscript, my wife, Shelagh.

2nd Edition: Contributing to the modifications and additions in the 2nd Edition are the many patients and veterinary contacts that it has been my pleasure and honour to know in the intervening years.

Preface

This book is planned as an introductory work on homoeopathy for use by veterinary surgeons and pet owners. This has been a difficult compromise but very necessary on account of the wide demand for homoeopathy and the gross shortage of veterinary surgeons practising this form of medicine. Some sections will therefore be beyond the pet owners and others will necessarily appear too obvious to veterinary surgeons. It is expected that veterinary surgeons well versed in the use of homoeopathy will want a more detailed reference section than this book contains but those in their early days of homoeopathic treatment will find it, I hope, an easy work of reference and a source of encouragement. Pet owners should be able to glean from its pages a wealth of easy to use remedies for common ailments in their pets and it should help them to understand the workings of homoeopathy, when a veterinary surgeon's help should be sought and how best to help him to help the patient by close observation of symptoms.

A glance at the list of contents will show how the book is laid out, the brief notes in the list helping one to use the book for reference. Some sections will be especially of concern to veterinary surgeons and this will be obvious in the text. The book leaves out all reference to farm animals.

The 2nd Edition carries an expanded index, in order to enhance the book's reference value, and a greater degree of cross-referencing appears in the text for the same purpose. The development of ideas since the 1st Edition has produced some modifications and additions to the text. It is hoped that the reader will benefit from these changes.

List of Contents

a) Head and Face, b) Eyes, c) Ears, d) Nose, e) Mouth, f) Digestive System, g) Urinary System, h) Male Sexual System, i) Female Sexual System (including Breeding), j) Respiratory System, k) Heart, Circulation and Blood, l) Lymphatic System, m) Locomotor System, n) Skin, o) Nervous System, p) Endocrine System

APPENDIX:

Introduction

The publication of this book is set amid an atmosphere of change in the thinking man's attitude to medicine, agriculture, diet, industry and environment.

The industrial revolution, the birth of modern medical ideas and the new agriculture, all of the late eighteenth century together with the accelerated loss and destruction of the natural environment and the appearance of 'easy foods' of the twentieth century have all grown hand in hand with population growth and social change. They have allowed redistribution of wealth, longer life, recession of the classical killer diseases, vast food production capacity and liberation of the housewife for career or recreation. The environment has suffered as population, travel and industry have grown. Nowadays, towards the end of the twentieth century, there is a growing awareness of the consequences of these trends. We are looking more and more into old and new ways of by-passing the harmful side of these changes, that is: shrinking of the natural environment, industrial pollution, wide spread use of agricultural sprays and fertilisers, dietary impurities and drug side effects. It would be quite wrong, however, to swing entirely in the opposite direction to these trends, running into danger of throwing the baby out with the bath water. It would not be right to react so wholeheartedly to these modern trends that we lose all advances. We must try to find the middle road where all that modern science has given us for the good of mankind can be retained and pick the best of what are either old or newly found methods in agriculture and horticulture, medicine, diet and health to keep us sound in mind and body. For this reason one must wholeheartedly applaud efforts to make organic methods of farming more productive and profitable, efforts to research into the validity and mechanisms of natural medicines and efforts to eliminate from our diet that which is harmful.

There is growing public interest in these fields which must be encouraged since demand usually promotes supply and this gradual shedding of public apathy, this awakening of a desire for more careful management by the powers-that-be, can only, in the long run, produce a more healthy and thoughtful approach by those that are involved in scientific advances. There should be no war between the ideologies of natural medicine and conventional medicine be it in the veterinary or human field. There should be mutual understanding and cross-pollination of ideas. It is for these reasons that I have tried, in this book, to draw attention to the scope of the one form of natural medicine, homoeopathy, which I have had time to study and use. I still, very occasionally, use conventional veterinary medicine when I feel it necessary so to do, therefore I do not intend this book to be a condemnation of conventional medicine but, rather, an illustration of ways in which 'alternative' medicine can help the health of pets without unnecessary use of chemicals and drugs. There seems to be a regrettable trend in orthodox medicine to believe that such drugs as antibiotics and corticosteroids can control most problems. If this were really so, why are more and more new and 'better' antibiotics needed? Antibiotics have their place but it is not the very prominent place they are given at present, by many today. (see page 20).

In the first chapter explaining homoeopathy I have given many good reasons for using homoeopathy in place of conventional veterinary medicine. In some cases, conventional veterinary medicine can appear to achieve an equally good result and should not be totally dismissed. The reasons for use of this one (homoeopathic) system as opposed to another are not always an argument about which is the most effective method but a look into logic, the benefits and limitations of one method in a defined set of circumstances. I have attempted an objective assessment of principles; which approach led me to change to homoeopathy in the first place!

In the following chapters, I have tried to show the role of the veterinary surgeon, the pet owner and the animal itself in achieving a cure.

Although this book is a handy reference book it should be studied carefully throughout, since many underlying principles of homoeopathic medicine are discussed in its pages. Use only as a reference work defeats the philosophy of homoeopathy in that this system of medicine is not used to treat diseases as such, but rather the patient itself, according to its individual response to disease, i.e. according to the symptoms displayed. To look up, for instance, vomiting and its treatments in Chapter 8 and to use the remedy which seems immediately obvious, could fail to effect a cure as a result of failure to take the patient into account. It is in this field that veterinary surgeons can be essential to avoid needless suffering from protracted disease through wrong choices of remedy. By and large the chapter on veterinary involvement should act as a guide to where and when his help is necessary.

What is probably most confusing at first to those embarking on a study of homoeopathy is the naming of the remedies. These are listed at the end of the book with their common names. They are obtainable from various sources as described in Chapter 3 and should be carefully looked after according to a simple set of rules laid out in Chapter 7. A glossary can be found in the Appendix section to elucidate the more specialised terms used in this book and others.

A chapter of selected case histories is included in order to illustrate various points in the text and this should be read with a critical mind. Much can be learnt from the successes and failures of others.

Since the first edition of this book there have been many changes in attitudes to homoeopathy. The BMA published a report on alternative medicine which showed a remarkable lack of objectivity by a body supposedly guided by objective principles. The media have given homoeopathy, and other alternatives, tremendous exposure not least in the veterinary field. The public appear to be more and more aware of, interested in and looking for alternative therapies. The E.E.C. have outlawed growth promotion implants in beef and are addressing the problems of drug control on the farm. Farmers are taking to homoeopathy more than ever before. Veterinary surgeons are able to take official courses specially designed for them and leading to a qualification (the first of its kind in the world). The International Association for Veterinary Homoeopathy was formed in

Luxemburg in 1986 and serves as an unprecedented medium for the exchange of veterinary homoeopathy knowledge, skills and understanding not least through the pages of its International Journal for Veterinary Homoeopathy. Research is making new strides, serving to further the understanding and acceptance of homoeopathic principles. Membership of the British Association of Homoeopathic Veterinary Surgeons has more than trebled in the intervening years. I believe a new era of understanding is in the making.

CHAPTER I

Nature of Homoeopathy

All 'alternative' medicine practices tend to be lumped together in people's minds and homoeopathy is no exception. It is often confused with herbalism, faith healing, 'black box' medicine, radiaesthesia etc, which is not correct although perhaps some of them are related. All have a part to play but confusion of the systems serves no purpose. Homoeopathy is in reality one of the most scientific and precise forms of medicine available. This remark may seem difficult to justify but I hope to do so in this chapter, and the following chapters should serve to illustrate it.

Samuel Hahnemann in the late eighteenth century gave us formalised homoeopathy but the principle involved has been popping up in medical philosophy since Classical Greek times. Sadly it was never developed as a theory until Samuel Hahnemann's work by which time new lines of scientific medicine were being explored. This chronology had repercussions on the later acceptability of homocopathy. Up until this period medicine had been a very illogical hit and miss affair. It seemed that the more distasteful, pungent or unusual a medicine, the more effective it was expected to be. There appeared to be little regard for negative results and what cures did occur most probably occurred as a result of the patient's inner strength triumphing over both the disease and the 'cure'.

Discovery: Like Cures Like

Hahnemann became more and more disillusioned with medicine and turned more to his scholarly work of translating medical texts into German, this despite his renown and prominence in the medical world. It was while translating the Materia Medica by Cullen, a Scottish physician, that he embarked upon his adventure of discovery. He disagreed with Cullen's explanation of the action of Cinchona bark against malaria, one of the few effective treatments of those days. In trying to find out the mechanism he tested the drug on himself, producing malarial symptoms!

He added a footnote to his translation of Cullen's Materia Medica questioning the proposed 'tonic' effect on the stomach as follows (I have updated the language):

> *'By combining the strongest bitters and the strongest astringents we can obtain a compound which, in small doses, possesses a more powerful tonic effect on the stomach than Cinchona bark, and yet no fever specific can be made from such a compound. The undiscovered principle of the effect of Cinchona bark is not easy to find. I took, for several days as an experiment, four drams of China (Cinchona), twice daily. My feet and fingertips etc., at first became cold. I became languid and drowsy and then my heart began to palpitate; my pulse became quick and hard, and an intolerable anxiety, trembling, prostration in all the limbs, pulsation in the head, redness of cheeks, thirst, (the symptoms usually associated with intermittent fever – Malaria) all made their appearance. These symptoms lasted from two to three hours every time and recurred only when I repeated the dose. I discontinued the medicine and I was once more in good health.'*

This set his mind on the track of 'let like be cured by like' or 'similia similibus curentur'. Hahnemann writes of his newly discovered Natural Law:

> *'Every medicine which, among the symptoms it can cause in a healthy body, reproduces those most present in a given disease, is capable of curing the disease in the swiftest, most thorough and most enduring fashion.'*

Being a true scientist, having made this hypothesis he had to test it exhaustively. In twenty years he tested sixty-seven remedies on himself, family, friends and medical student volunteers. These substances were taken by many people and the results noted. The experiments were carried out under rigorous dietary and behavioural control. The noted results of major and minor symptoms were compiled into a 'Materia Medica' which, by listing what a substance could cause, was a treatise on what each substance could cure. He also wrote the first edition of 'The Organon of Medicine'.

This book, the summary of his theory and philosophy, was published in 1810 and it constitutes a remarkable exercise in logic.

He carried on his work and investigations tirelessly but could not accumulate enough evidence of medical cures using his system until the winter of 1812/13 when Napoleon's army was retreating across Europe and had lost the battle of Leipzig where Hahnemann lived. Here Hahnemann treated 180 cases of Typhus in the disease-ridden stragglers and only two died, one of these a very old man. Later in his life, one of his students also proved the potential of this system on a large scale. In 1831 there was an epidemic of Cholera and in Raab this doctor treated 154 cases and lost six (3.9%). Orthodox doctors treating 1500 cases between them lost 821 (54.7%). These results speak for themselves. (Both episodes preceded the knowledge of bacteria or antibiotics, which raises the question whether this knowledge is vitally important for the cure of disease.)

Potency

The tests of substances on healthy people, 'the provings'*, were only one part of his amazing discoveries. The second part was that as he set about to find the minimum dose necessary for a cure, he found that the more dilute he made his remedies the more effective they became. This method of serial dilution and succussion (his method of vigourously mixing the diluted remedies at each stage) he called potentisation. He wrote:

> '*The very smallest doses of medicines chosen for the homoeopathic diseases are each a match for the corresponding disorder. The Physician will choose a homoeopathic remedy in just so small a dose as will overcome the disease*'.

Conventional medicine whether using antiopathy (the treatment by opposites to neutralise a disease symptom) or allopathy (the treatment by an unrelated substance to try to alter the body's response to disease) is totally different in this respect. If one dilutes below the usual dose efficacy is

---

Poorly translated from the German: Prüfing – a test.

lost. Thus Hahnemann's discovery of the ability to use infinitely dilute solutions has allowed us to use immeasurably low doses of a substance to effect a cure. We can use some of nature's most powerfully poisonous substances, such as arsenic or snake venoms, to effect most dramatic curative processes without the need to worry about potential toxicity.

Allopathy and Antiopathy

Hahnemann wrote so vehemently against the illogical Allopaths of his day (those that used substances unrelated to the disease) that he turned the conventional school of medical opinion drastically against him. Thus the acceptance of his theories of homoeopathy was limited. Nowadays, conventional medicine has eliminated those irrelevant and harmful practices from its repertoire, so it no longer needs to smart under the worst of Hahnemann's criticisms of allopathy, but it still has to contend with Hahnemann's criticisms of antiopathy. Most of modern conventional medicine (wrongly termed allopathy) is antiopathy, that is, the treatment of a disease symptom with an agent designed to neutralise that symptom. Examples of this are corticosteroids to suppress inflammation, pain killers to suppress pain, purgatives to combat constipation and binding agents to counteract diarrhoea. These medicines have a logic* but against that one has Hahnemann's arguments against suppression of symptoms and his justifications for treatment by 'like' substances. He states and this is hard to contradict:

> *'Important symptoms of persistent diseases have never been treated with such palliative, antagonistic remedies without the opposite state, a relapse – indeed a palpable aggravation – of the malady occuring hours afterwards' (6th edition of the Organon).*

He again quotes and this must be deemed still true today:

> *'For a persistent tendency to sleepiness during the day the physician prescribed coffee, and when it had exhausted its action*

---

* Based on the principle of palliation

4

the day-somnolence increased. For frequent waking at night he gave in the evening, without heeding the other symptoms of the disease, Opium, which by virtue of its primary action produced the same night (dull, stupified) sleep, but the subsequent nights were still more sleepless than before.'

He also uses the same logic against the antiopathic treatment of diarrhoea or constipation. This is all stated for humans but the same applies in veterinary usage. Who has not seen the suppression of a dog's itch by corticosteroid therapy and the subsequent recurrence with renewed vigour after the therapy has worn off? He even postulated that some cancers arise from continued suppression of disease symptoms. The case history (on p. 148) of the rodent ulcer illustrates a similar point.

Sadly today's conventional (antiopathic) medicine has inherited the discredited and obsolete allopath's suspicion and animosity towards Hahnemann's homoeopathic theory. Despite its painstakingly scientific origins, and despite Hahnemann's unerring powers of observation, modern scientific medicine cannot accept his findings. A look at contemporary medical breakthroughs shows us what a sad loss it is to us all that Hahnemann's discoveries could not have gone side by side with the scientific developments of those times, which have preceded today's conventional medicine.

The chronological list shows an increasing preoccupation with the details of scientific theory and development and had they been coupled with Hahnemann's logic (worked out, as can be seen, way ahead of his time – his results long predating any realistic expectation of success by modern medical standards) would have given us an unparalleled composite medical theory. This is still to come if the power of scientific thought can be directed at an analysis of Hahnemannian principles.

460–375 BC – HIPPOCRATES: Origins of a rational approach to
(approx.)   medicine, writings rediscovered only in the Middle
              Ages, reputed references to theory of 'like-cures-like'.
129–200 AD – GALEN: Rational approach to anatomy – lost until 1540.
1540   – VESALIUS: Builds on Galen's work.
1628   – HARVEY: Theories of blood circulation.
1680's   – LEEUWENHOEK: Discovery of bacteria although
              they were not recognised as being involved in disease.

1753	– LIND: Discovery that scurvy is preventable by inclusion of fruit and fresh vegetables in diet.
1755	– BIRTH OF HAHNEMANN
1755	– BLACK: ⎰ Discovery of gases which make up air
1766	– CAVENDISH: ⎱ (oxygen and hydrogen).
1773	– HUNTER: Changes approach to surgery.
1781–1785	– PRIESTLY/CAVENDISH/LAVOISIER: Discover composition of water.
1784	– HAHNEMANN: First medical essay, denouncing bad medical practices of his day, praising veterinary surgeons and natural medicine.
1785–1795	– FOUNDING of veterinary profession in England.
1790	– HAHNEMANN: Work on Cinchona bark, evolution of Homoeopathy.
1790	– SPALLANZANI: Non-spontaneous generation of microbes (still not concerned with disease).
1790's	– GROWTH OF HOMOEOPATHIC MATERIA MEDICA
1791	– HUNTER: Involved in uprating veterinary profession.
1793	– NEW VETERINARY COLLEGE: Denounces 'quackery' in English veterinary surgery.
1795	– HAHNEMANN: Essays on value of sleep, clothing, social medicine, sanitation, fresh air, fresh water, exercise and diet; and of the ills of poverty, lack of family, education etc. (These ideas were very much ahead of their time when put in this chronological list).
1796	– JENNER: First vaccination (related to Isopathy?)
1810–1843	– SUCCESSIVE EDITIONS OF HAHNEMANN'S 'ORGANON'.
1811–1821	– SUCCESSIVE PARTS OF HAHNEMANN'S 'MATERIA MEDICA PURA' PUBLISHED.
1811	– AVOGADRO: Atomic Theory.
1813	– HAHNEMANN: Treatment of Typhus in Leipzig, curing an incredible 178 cases out of 180. One of those to die was a very old man. Nothing was yet known of bacterial involvement in disease or of hygiene or of antibiotics.
1824	– DUTROCHET: See 1839.
1828	– HAHNEMANN: 'Chronic diseases; their peculiar nature and their homoeopathic cure' published.
1831	– OUTBREAK OF CHOLERA in Raab. Homoeopathy loses 6 out of 154 (4%). Conventional medicine of the day loses 821 out of 1501 (55%). HAHNEMANN, with reference to the epidemic of cholera sweeping Europe, gave very advanced advice on ventilation, hygiene, sterilisation, infection and quarantine:

'In order to make the infection and spread of cholera impossible, the garments, linen etc. of all strangers have to be kept in

quarantine (whilst their bodies were cleansed with speedy baths and provided with clean clothes) and retained there for two hours at stove heat of 80°C – this represents a heat at which all known infectious matters and consequently the living miasmas are annihilated.'

'The most stinking infections took place and made astounding progress whenever in the stuffy places of ships, filled as they are with musty aqueous vapours, the Cholera miasma found an element favourable to its own multiplication and throve to an enormously increased swarm of those infinitely small, invisible living organisms which are murderously hostile to human life and which most probably form the infectious matter of Cholera'.

It is surprising that Hahnemann has written a very up-to-date (although strangely worded) advisory document on the prevention of Cholera. The ideas incorporated (when put in modern language with medical jargon corrected) are well able to stand up to modern medical theory despite the fact that half a century was still to pass before the basis of that theory was laid down. (Pasteur, Lister, Koch etc.). Still more surprising. perhaps is that Hahnemann was able to cure by homoeopathy without recourse to those medical theories! He pre-empted the theories, used them for prevention and used his own homoeopathic theory for cure.

1833	– FARADAY: Laws for electricity and magnetism.
1835	– BASSI: Microbes cause disease in silkworms – his work was not widely accepted!
1837	– MÜLLER: Discovers the function of nerves.
1839	– SCHWANN & SCHLIEDEN: Cell theory expanded from 1824.
1843	– DEATH OF HAHNEMANN.
1846	– MORTON: Anaesthetic ether vapour.
1853	– FLORENCE NIGHTINGALE: Pioneered nursing.
1854–1856	– FLORENCE NIGHTINGALE: Put theories into practice in Crimea.
1864	– PASTEUR: Germ theory of disease – methods of sterilisation. Ironically Pasteur finally swayed the arguments whether germs caused disease or were incidental to disease. Homoeopathy recognises both concepts with the emphasis on the latter. Modern medicine does too but the emphasis is on the former.
1865	– LISTER: Pioneered antiseptics – Carbolic.
1865	– BERNARD: Principles of scientific investigation. Also theories on the body's internal environment. The start of hormone theory.
1866	– MENDEL: Fundamental laws of inheritance.
1877	– MANSON: Discovered the spread of disease by insect vectors.
1882	– BERI BERI DISEASE: Controlled in Japanese navy by reducing rice in diet, this tied in with Lind 1753.

1882	– KOCH: Discovered the Tubercle Bacillus.
1883	– KOCH: Discovered the Cholera agent. (So long after Hahnemann's writings see 1831).
1880's	– PASTEUR: Vaccines for Rabies and Anthrax. This and Jenner's work were enlightened shots in the dark, viruses were yet to be discovered.
1884	– KOLLER: Local anaesthetic – Cocaine.
1886	– KOCH: Methods of study of bacteria, theories of vaccination and infection. These were evolved in yet another Cholera epidemic in Europe.
1887	– BUIST: First sees a virus but does not recognise it for what it is (Cowpox virus).
1891	– MURRAY: First hormone extract (Thyroid).
1892	– IWANOWSKI: Filtrable agent caused Tobacco Mosaic disease (a step towards discovering viruses).
1895	– RONTGEN: Discovered X-rays.
1898	– BEIJERINCK: Discovered virus.
1900	– ROSS & MANSON: Proved that the Malaria parasite is spread by the mosquito. This was the disease on which Hahnemann first embarked on his homoeopathic adventure.
1902	– BAYLISS & STARLING: First use of the word 'hormone'.
1900's	– CURIE: Discovered Radium and its ability to suppress cancer, sterilise bacteria etc.
1903	– BUCHNER: Discovered enzymes in yeast.
1906	– PASCHEN: Rediscovered Small Pox virus.
1929	– FLEMING: Penicillin, the first antibiotic.
1929	– WOODRUFF & GOODPASTURE: Discovered Fowl Pox virus.
1931	– WOODRUFF & GOODPASTURE: Culture viruses in eggs, laying down the foundation of modern virus vaccine production.
1932	– KING & WAUGH: Isolated the first vitamin (C).
1935	– STANLEY: Crystallised viruses.
1935	– DISCOVERY OF SULPHONAMIDES in chemotherapy. This was a useful addition to Penicillin and together they still form the basis of modern antibacterial therapy.
1939	– FIRST VIRUS SEEN under electron microscope.
1940	– LARGE SCALE USE of Penicillin.

Since then a horde of drugs acting at the cellular level have been discovered and manufactured. Modern medicine and homoeopathy really started to diverge in the second half of the nineteenth century owing to the deluge of scientific discoveries occurring from then onwards.

What a shame that Hahnemann, who evolved a system of medicine that required no name for a disease, no indentification of bacteria or viruses and no knowledge of cellular chemistry or physiology should work in one direction while the rest of the medical world worked in a direction of the study of disease from the point of view of disease agents, cellular mechanisms and physiological and biochemical pathways*. The two were idealogically unable to work together. Much has been lost as a result and for this Hahnemann must be held largely responsible for he was unbridled in his attacks on conventional medical men and showed an arrogance and self-righteousness which could not endear him to any but devout disciples.

The Way Forward

What is needed today is a selection from the best of both worlds. One needs Hahnemann's insight into the nature of disease, his painstaking methods and his taut principles coupled with the enquiring mind of the modern scientist. Let us look at one of Hahnemann's own comments against the illogical allopaths of his day:

> 'To render (through ignorance) if not fatal, at all events incurable, the vast majority of all diseases, namely those of a chronic character, by continually weakening and tormenting the debilitated patient, already suffering without that, from his disease and by adding new destructive drug diseases, this clearly seems to be the unhallowed main business of the old school of medicine (allopathy) and a very easy business it is when one has become an adept in this pernicious practice, and is sufficiently insensible to the stings of conscience.'

Charming words indeed! Little wonder the medical world turned against him. Take however his positive side:

> 'The physician's high and only mission is to restore the sick to health, to cure as it is termed. The highest ideal of cure is rapid, gentle and permanent restoration of health; or removal and annihilation of the disease in its whole extent, in the shortest, most reliable, and most harmless way on easily comprehensible principles.
>
> If the physician clearly perceives what is to be cured in diseases, if he clearly perceives what is curative in each medicine and if he knows how to adapt, according to clearly defined principles, what is curative in medicines to what he had discovered to be

---

* See also Chapter 15 and Appendix 8.

morbid in the patient – to adapt it as well in respect of suitability of medicines as also in respect to the proper dose and the proper period for repeating the dose:– If, finally, he knows the obstacles to recovery in each case and is aware how to remove them, so that the restoration may be permanent, then he understands how to treat judiciously and rationally, and he is a true practitioner of the healing art.'

We do well to remember these principles today whether doctors or veterinary surgeons. In fact it is encouraging to know that Hahnemann thought very highly of veterinary surgeons and their clinical prowess especially in their treatment of ulcers (still a very difficult clinical problem). He wrote:

'In spite of this my pride does not prevent me from confessing that veterinary surgeons are usually more successful, that is, have more skill in the treatment of old wounds than the most learned professors and members of the academics – I wish I had their skill based on experience, which they have frequently only acquired through treating animals.'

(From his first essay 1784 'Directions for curing old sores and ulcers'). The same essay – written 6 years before his discovery of homoeopathy – makes recommendation for a reversion to natural medicine:

'Their importance draws the conscientious physician more and more to simple nature amidst the rejoicing of his patients'.

It is interesting to note that ethically minded veterinary surgeons in the dawning of their official profession in England also denounced the quackery to be found in the surgery performed by the vagrant 'farrier vets' of the day. To be fair it is right to quote alongside Hahnemann's praise of vets in the medicine department this vehement condemnation of some of their number in the surgery department.

'If we observe the dangerous practice of farriers, in their surgical operation, we shall see them daily sacrificing horses, by boldly mangling the original parts of the body, without knowing anything of its structure. How many muscles, and tendons, divided cross-ways, veins opened, nerves destroyed, membranes torn and essential organs more or less affected, by the ignorant

boldness of these unskilled operators, whose reputation has been supported merely by public supineness and credulity!' (1791).

Strong words were obviously not Hahnemann's copyright! Happily surgery has progressed greatly since these times, thanks in great part to the work of John Hunter in the human and veterinary fields.

What is Homoeopathy?

Homoeopathy is the selection of a substance to cure a disease by the knowledge that the same substance could cause symptoms similar to those seen in the patient (see p. 1). For examples of what symptoms can be cured by which substances I refer you to Chapters 8 et seq.

Also now an accepted part of Homoeopathy is the principle of the minimal dose (see pp. 3, 178). The substances used are diluted serially either in 1/10th stages (decimal dilutions) or 1/100th stages (centesimal dilutions) which are designated x and c potencies respectively. Thus Arnica 30c is tincture of Arnica diluted one in a hundred, thirty times or a dilution of 10^{-60}. Arnica 6x is tincture of Arnica diluted one in ten, six times, that is, a dilution of 10^{-6}. Succussion is carried out at each stage and it is this which seems to release the curative energy of the substance, while the successive dilution removes its toxic or harmful effects. Homoeopathic remedies can therefore be used in the confidence that, even if the wrong remedy is chosen, while it will achieve no cure it will do no harm.[*]

The principles governing choice of remedy are outlined in Chapter 5 and some leading guides are to be found in Chapters 8-14, so it suffices to reiterate here that in order to gain a cure by homoeopathy one must obtain as close a match of disease symptoms to symptoms in the materia medica as one possibly can. I will discuss the limitations this imposes on veterinary homoeopathy in Chapter 5. It is important to remember, however, that a patient exhibits a totality of symptoms whether they be behavioural, physical or mental; symptoms of the whole body or only a part of it (the so called 'generals' and 'particulars' of homoeopathy); or whether they be common symptoms or rarer 'peculiar'

*But see footnote p. 38.

ones. Thus treating a patient homoeopathically implies a treatment of the whole patient not just a diseased part. This allows a patient's own individual reaction to a disease (that reaction constitutes a symptom) to influence one's choice of remedy for that patient. One does not therefore treat a named disease but the totality of symptoms representing that individual patient, therefore two patients with the same named disease will often be given different remedies. This individuality in response to a disease, (which undoubtedly occurs) is what often confuses conventional medicine which is reliant on diagnosis of a named disease (a named disease is supposed to give uniform identifiable symptoms and receive uniform treatment). The picture is also confused when a conventional medicine is given in that a patient also responds, with its own individual sensitivity, to that medicine. Homoeopathy not only allows for this it demands a knowledge of it.

As can be understood from the history of homoeopathy (p. 2.), as a form of medicine it has depended for its data upon 'provings' in people. These people were volunteers. This has always been the case and is still going on today. Animal experimentation in the evaluation of medicines has therefore not played a part and is not necessary for the practice of human homoeopathy. This has endeared it to many who deplore the use of experimental animals in conventional medicine whether for human or veterinary use. However, this imposes limitations on the use of homoeopathy for veterinary purposes as has been outlined in Chapter 5. This limitation is imposed by the fact that we must assume a similarity of symptoms produced by a remedy whether in humans or different species of animals. This could hold true for some but certainly not all of our remedies. 'Field trials' in veterinary work, (careful trial work carried out on populations of farm animals and pets in the normal course of veterinary work, as opposed to laboratory conditions) are providing useful data while still adhering to the humane traditions of homoeopathy, but the problems of species differences still do apply.

Mechanism of Homoeopathy

Since one is using a remedy similar in its action to the disease itself and the principle isolated in the remedy is probably, owing to the dilution/succussion process (potentisation), a form of energy, the homoeopathic remedy most probably acts upon the body's system in the same way as the disease but in a more powerful manner eclipsing the disease. If one takes the homoeopath's view that disease (literally dis-ease or ill at ease) is a dynamic disturbance of the body (rather than an entity in itself as conventional medicine implies) then what is better than a remedy of purely dynamic quality? Since it is thought that it is only energy its effect in the body is unlikely to last forever and is therefore easily eliminated from the system so that its own disease producing ability is never realised. (See Chapter 6 figs 2–6 for further thoughts on this subject.) I quote from Samuel Hahnemann:

> '*A weaker dynamic affection is permanently extinguished in the living organism by a stronger one, if the latter (whilst differing in kind) is very similar to the former in its manifestations.*'

He goes on eloquently (as always) to establish why homoeopathic medicines are more powerful than the disease agents they are to combat.

The Homoeopath's theory of disease and its cure is therefore lifted straight from the writings of Samuel Hahnemann. He postulated:

a) A vital force within a patient.
b) A disease is a morbid influence upon that vital force.
c) The symptoms are an expression of the reaction of that vital force to disease influence.
d) An effective medicine is one which mimics those symptoms when applied to the vital force.
e) It is a more powerful influence than the disease.
f) It overpowers the disease unleashing the vital force's full power to extinguish the new temporary influence and restore the patient to health.

An analogy can be drawn with brute force and judo as methods of self defence.

To apply a force opposite to the aggressor, if the aggressor is strong, will fail, whereas if only one applies a force in the same direction as the aggressor (the art of judo) a very powerful adversary can be defeated with small use of force. This superficially, is the strength of homoeopathy.

The homoeopath's concept of cure of disease is summarised:

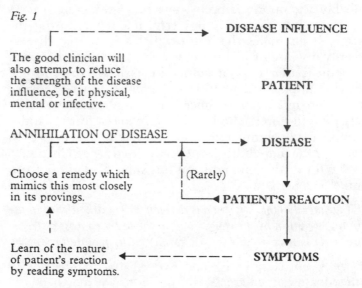

Fig. 1

DISEASE INFLUENCE

The good clinician will
also attempt to reduce
the strength of the disease
influence, be it physical,
mental or infective.

PATIENT

ANNIHILATION OF DISEASE

DISEASE

Choose a remedy which
mimics this most closely
in its provings.

(Rarely)

PATIENT'S REACTION

Learn of the nature
of patient's reaction
by reading symptoms.

SYMPTOMS

Dotted lines are disease–mitigating pathways. (See also p. 103).

Rational Discussion of Common Criticisms of the Homoeopathic Method

1 It is argued that homoeopaths do not understand how their remedies work so how can they, as scientifically trained professional people, use them? It can be said that once accepting that what a substance can cause it can also cure then one can postulate the way a homoeopathic remedy works. It is thought to work by mimicking exactly, or very closely, the dynamic disease process in the body and over-powering it in its own sphere of action. The remedy, being only energy, then fades and the body is cured of its disease process; the symptoms then cease. This does not constitute knowledge or full understanding but how much more can it be said that we fail to understand the workings of modern drugs? Who can foretell the side effects of new drugs? They are often tested in unrelated species. Homoeopathic remedies for the human are tested in humans. They can be tested, on the same humane basis, in animals.

14

2 It is argued that so-called cures by homoeopathic treatments are not proven, because:

a) They are not evaluated in proper trials,
b) The condition could have self-cured at the same time as the treatment was applied,
c) The diagnosis could have been incorrect.

We may respond rationally by saying:

a) Trials are in progress in man and animals under field conditions and are proving very promising.
b) There are too many coincidences of this kind to accept this hypothesis for the curing of so many cases. This and the next argument could just as easily be levelled at any form of medicine, including the conventional system.
c) The diagnosis can always be incorrect since human judgement is involved. However, taking a great many cases where orthodox clinicians have satisfied themselves with a diagnosis indicating surgery, incurability or euthanasia, apparent cures have been effected by use of homoeopathy. The diagnosis could still have been wrong since no clinician is infallible but the orthodox clinician was satisfied to the extent that euthanasia or surgery would have been carried out but for homoeopathic intervention.

3 It is often said that the doses used ensure that no material substance is present in the remedy, therefore no cure is possible. Here one can only ask: What do we know of what is curative in a substance? Need it be a material part of that substance or an energy pattern derived from that substance for instance? Again trial work shows that it does work so we need to rethink our ideas on drug mechanisms to suit the new evidence.

4 The placebo effect is often said to be the mechanism behind the apparent cures. This is the means whereby a patient can be cured by the psychological benefit of receiving a treatment whatever that treatment may be. In other words the patient is humoured to such an extent by receiving a treatment however ineffective or inapplicable, that his body's mechanisms effect a self-cure. This could be true in humans but surely is unlikely to occur in animals and therefore veterinary homoeopathy has discounted this criticism. It is an interesting point that those who condemn homoeopathy as having no demonstrable mechanism can accept the placebo effect without question. Surely the placebo effect (a well-proven phenomenon) is proof enough of the body's mysterious healing powers? Secondly homoeopathic treatment often works in cases when other treatments have failed. Surely were the placebo effect the mechanism here then it would have operated already, prior to the homoeopathic treatment?

5 It is also said that homoeopathy is not levelled at the supposed root cause of the disease e.g. bacteria, or the cellular or humoral mechanisms involved in the disease process, and therefore has no hope of achieving a cure. Here again, if one hypothesises that disease is not necessarily caused by bacteria, etc, but that these in many cases may be incidental to disease and that deviations of cellular and humoral pathways are but a part of the symptoms of (that is, the patient's reaction to) the disease then why does one need to focus one's attentions upon them however interesting such a study might be? Treat the patient and these symptoms and opportune invaders will perish.

6 It can be said, perhaps that a patient coming to a homoeopathic physician has faith in that physician and therefore a cure results. The same argument applies as in number 4, animals surely disprove this theory.

7 It could be argued that homoeopathic remedies, unbeknown to the homoeopath, contain an impurity which is an accidental curative agent applicable to the disease in question.

a) Homoeopathic pharmacies are under strict governmental legislative control as are conventional pharmacies and this therefore becomes unlikely.

b) As can be seen in Chapters 8–14, the remedies are successfully used each against a wide spectrum of symptoms. Surely no accidental ingredient could achieve the results claimed of the correctly chosen homoeopathic remedy against such a wealth of seemingly unrelated symptoms in unrelated organs? Secondly the same accidental ingredient would be very unlikely to appear in all batches of any one remedy therefore one would be totally unable to achieve consistent results were an accidental ingredient the effective portion. Thirdly, why would a remedy chosen by the similia principle appear to work when an irrelevant remedy fails if it is only an accidental ingredient which is effective? This ingredient should by law of averages appear in any remedy and therefore any remedy is just as likely to work.

None of these rational arguments is intended to decry conventional antiopathic medicine. They are all intended to infuse the essential ingredient of logic into any discussion on homoeopathy. By careful logic alone should we be guided in our research for the ultimate healing truth. This must be our quest if we are to aspire to Hahnemann's idea of a physician's mission (p. 9).

Why Use Homoeopathy?

This chapter has not served its purpose at all if it has not shown the peculiarities of homoeopathy that make it a very sensible choice of treatment in animals whenever the similia principle can be established. The following points can serve to reiterate its main points:–

1 No side effects (See p. 38 and p. 46 however).

2 No suppression of symptoms, for later more vicious reappearance.

3 No dependence on diagnosis but only a dependence on symptom observation.
   This not only allows one to treat animals with no diagnosable disease, but also enables one to tackle a new disease as yet not classified in terms of agents and prescribed treatments. Recent cases in point are Parvo-virus in dogs and Key-Gaskell Syndrome in cats.[†]

4 No need for laboratory trials in animals for the proving of medicines.

5 Allowance for and dependence on a patient's individuality.

† *At time of 1st Edition.*

17

6 Whole patient treatment; it is often said in the consulting room after a course of homoeopathic treatment that the patient has 'never been better'. This implies a deeper effect of the remedy than one might expect, acting on the whole patient not just on the superficial symptoms of disease. (The wholistic concept is justified by the phenomenon).

7 Homoeopathy appears to work with the body's own disease-combating mechanisms to effect a cure and this constitutes a most natural, humane and effective method of cure.

8 No environmental pollution.

9 Ability to treat the foetus in utero preventing the effects of illness of the dam and miasmic effect. (Eugenics.)

10 In farm animals, no food residues.

Now please read on and enjoy the following chapters which attempt to act as a guide to the practical use of homoeopathic remedies in the veterinary application. Please may I exhort you all to purchase Arnica and use it according to the guidelines described in the relevant parts of Chapters 8-14, in order firstly to get a feel for the use of homoeopathic remedies (Arnica is so frequently indicated that one will be using it often), and secondly to convince yourself of the far-reaching and often astonishing effects of homoeopathy upon the expected course of the conditions described, had you not used the remedy. I also refer you to page 28. Chapter 3, in this connection.

CHAPTER 2

When To Call The Vet

Not for nothing has your veterinary surgeon undergone five or six years of rigorous training. His accumulated knowledge on the variability, scope and effect of disease, his ability to assess seriousness of a case, his ability to institute such correct dietary, supportive, nursing and management procedures as can aid a cure are all to be greatly respected, *whether or not he practices homoeopathy*. It is also notably difficult to be objective about one's own family and the same applies to one's pets. The veterinary surgeon can provide the valuable objectivity needed. I commend you to re-read Hahnemann's words quoted on p. 9. These words call for a high level of dedication and understanding. Only by repeated practice, constant reading, constant harsh lessons of experience and experience of the sheer variety of reaction to disease shown by a multiplicity of patients is the veterinary surgeon able to be aware of what is to be cured in disease (that is noticing all the symptoms). Only by these same lessons and experiences can he be aware of what is curative in medicines (that is, the 'provings' in the Materia Medica). Only by constant practice can he learn to match symptoms to provings, choose the correct remedy, dose at the required level, at the required frequency for an adequate duration. Only through his training and experience can he learn the nursing and management tricks necessary to 'removing the obstacles to recovery'. Although Hahnemann is talking about the practice of homoeopathy, conventional veterinary medicine has much to offer in this respect and owners should not lightly undertake the treatment of their own animals.

This is not to say that pet owners, safe in the knowledge that homoeopathic medicines have no side effects, cannot usefully set to work to cure their own pet using guidelines set down in this book and using the handy reference chapters on diseases and remedies (Chapters 8–14). However, what they must try to do is to be aware of what is dangerous in the way of disease and what is not dangerous, what is serious and what is not so serious. What is acute and what is chronic. What will benefit from veterinary help and what absolutely requires it. What requires immediate action and what is not so desperate. All this seems to be asking rather a lot but most of it should be instinctive. One must learn how to let instincts come to the surface of awareness. Those who have experience of children and their ailments should know what is meant by all these considerations. A child (especially a very young one) is very similar in the problems set for a parent and his doctor to a pet and the problems it sets for its owner and its veterinary surgeon. The dramatic effect upon the demeanour of child or pet by acute diseases, the lack of communication about symptoms, the concern felt by parent or owner, all are very similar. Since so many people have contact with children in health and sickness this should give them confidence to deal more certainly with their pet's ailments. The human race has deeply rooted instincts in relation to management of disease in its children. These should be given full rein when it comes to considering one's pets' problems.

In Chapters 8–14, those conditions where veterinary help should most certainly be sought are marked as such. Other conditions can reasonably be considered for treatment at home. Also remember that no condition is so serious that a home remedy, immediately administered, can do harm and in many cases a lot of good may derive. Although, in many cases, conventional veterinary medicine can counteract a homoeopathic remedy given at home, there are no cases where a homoeopathic remedy can conflict with the conventional treatment to the detriment of the patient.

Now to apply logic to determine the kind of conditions wherein homoeopathy alone should not be used whether by veterinary surgeon or pet owner. That is not to say that homoeopathy will not help in such cases, it almost certainly will, since most of these conditions do not confine their effect to the locality of the body in which they occur but have a general effect as well. Consider them in more detail and this will become clear.

The first type to be considered are those rare conditions

where a bacterial infection is running its course in such a violent manner as to render the 'vital force' more or less unable to fight back. If a homoeopathic remedy alone is used under these circumstances – however correct that remedy might be – the condition may go on unabated, owing to the tremendous hold the bacterial infection has e.g. Meningitis, acute septicaemia, leptospiral jaundice. If however the appropriate antibiotic is given (the domain of the veterinary surgeon who alone understands the factors affecting choice and administration of these medicines) the downward trend in the patient can be reversed, releasing the 'vital force' from this stranglehold and leaving room for the appropriate homoeopathic remedy to effect a complete and lasting cure. In this manner one is using (as suggested in the introduction to this book) the best of both worlds. One cannot, in one's right mind, adhere to homoeopathy and shut out modern scientific developments to the detriment of the patient and not be accused of gross folly or neglect. It is possible that those who are totally proficient in homoeopathy can minimise the use of antibiotic or do without it altogether but *unless one has that skill and confidence* the patient must not be jeopardised.

Another set of circumstances where one cannot sit back and leave it to homoeopathy is the realm of injury. Again there are valuable homoeopathic remedies which can be relied upon to restore health in cases of minor injury (see Chapters 8–14) and help tremendously in cases of major injury (who can deny the marvellous effects of Arnica for instance) but again one would be sadly neglecting one's duty if one failed to staunch the flow of blood from a wound by appropriate methods, stitch a large wound to aid healing, immobilize a fracture or severe sprain to prevent pain and further damage, remove an injurious foreign body if this is necessary to recovery, replace dislocations, use surgery to repair any internal damage that is preventing recovery or institute measures to prevent any external influence which can impede the healing process. If one fails to do these one fails to fulfil the resolutions laid down on p. 9 of Chapter 1. It would not do harm to read these resolutions again now. A veterinary surgeon is bound by these as rules of his profession but a pet owner who takes upon himself the medical cure of his pet must also take these resolutions to heart, calling for help when needed. He becomes, for the moment, the 'physician' to whom Hahnemann refers, but must know when to refer the patient to a qualified person.

A third circumstance where, again, one should not lean entirely on homoeopathy, is the field of necessary surgery. Congenital reparable defects should be repaired by the appropriate surgical method if they constitute a threat to the animal's health. Abdominal catastrophes must be dealt with in the appropriate manner e.g. a swallowed foreign body (many cannot pass), intussusception (many will not self correct), abdominal adhesions which produce malfunction of the bowel and many other circumstances of a like nature. Physiological dysfunction of the bowel can probably be corrected non-surgically by the appropriate homoeopathic methods. Cancerous growths should be removed if they constitute an immediate threat to health or life (rather than rely on homoeopathy to cure such growths) at the same time using a homoeopathic remedy to correct the state of the 'vital force' which is predisposed to this condition in the first place. There may be no substitute to surgery to correct anatomical defects bred into an animal by successive malpractice of some early animal breeders. Such defects include ear or eye deformities of spaniels and blood hounds and leg deformities of many miniature breeds.

It is sometimes necessary as a last resort to institute major surgery such as castration or ovarohysterectomy to correct a condition which fails (for whatever reason) to respond to homoeopathy but again the appropriate homoeopathic remedy will prove an invaluable aid to recovery. It is not always necessary to resort to surgery to correct dental problems or urethral obstruction or to relieve severe impacted constipation by mechanical means, a homoeopathic remedy may effect a cure; but undue delay or experimentation is not to be encouraged. These conditions can be very serious if left unrelieved, especially urinary obstruction. As can be seen, veterinary attention is very much to be recommended in all the aforementioned circumstances.

In nearly all cases of surgery another non-homoeopathic procedure is required, that of anaesthesia, in this procedure, one unashamedly resorts to drug usage, with all its attendant side effects, in order to achieve humanity. It is in fact illegal to carry out surgery without appropriate anaesthesia and rightly so in the light of medical knowledge. Acupuncture is said to act as a substitute in China but is little used in this country as yet. Homoeopathy can be used to lessen the side effects and after effects of anaesthetics and should be used, but one day acupuncture may supercede drug anaesthesia.

When the vital force is no longer able to fight a disease influence, and a terminal situation has been reached, then exploitation of the undoubted palliative effects of drugs may be justified if there is still a chance for reasonable quality of life thereby. Side effects of drugs in these sad situations are a purely academic consideration since life is not expected to be long.

The author hopes in this chapter to have illustrated the place of veterinary advice, the place of veterinary skills and the place of non-homoeopathic methods. One is left, in the final instance, to make one's own decision whether or not to consult a veterinary surgeon but one must remember when in doubt – consult. Veterinary surgeons often ask the advice of colleagues too! The most important single contribution the veterinary surgeon is able to make for you and your pet is his ability to carry out a full examination including observation and evaluation of symptoms and history. His training and experience give him a tremendous lead over anyone who tries to do this without the advantage of training. This cannot be underestimated. If it is humanly possible to avoid mistreatment and mismanagement of a case by failure to notice important symptoms then it is more likely that the veterinary surgeon will avoid it than the untrained, however enlightened and intelligent, lay person. To further illustrate these points I refer you to Chapters 4/5/6.

It is not my place to discuss veterinary professional ethics in this book but it is worth reminding both homoeopathic veterinary surgeons and pet owners that homoeopathic medicine in animals is still veterinary medicine even if it uses no drugs as we understand the word. A case referred to a homoeopathic veterinary surgeon after conventional treatment still requires, for the good of the patient, the customary inter-veterinary communication. Otherwise one fails in one's duty to learn all one can of the patient. It is also to be recommended that veterinary surgeons do not yield to the temptation, put in their paths by distance, to prescibe *without first seeing the patient* so that he can, in the best veterinary and homoeopathic traditions, extract as much information from the history-taking sessions as he possibly can. There are, sadly, still times when homoeopathy fails to achieve a cure. This is almost certainly due not to the patient's failure to respond to homoeopathy but more to one's inability to correctly read all the symptoms and history. I refer you to Chapter 5 on selection of remedy to explain this statement and the limitations imposed on veterinary homoeopathy by the animal's inability to talk! This makes it very important to use one's diagnostic ability to the utmost and distance is not conducive to increasing one's chances of success.

If you wish to visit a veterinary surgeon using homoeopathy it is advisable to ascertain whether that veterinarian is well enough versed in homoeopathy to be able to take on the particular problem and species concerned. When visiting a veterinarian for a homoeopathic second opinion it will be necessary to provide a full case history from your own original veterinarian. This is a routine event for veterinary surgeons and every veterinarian is obliged to help you in this way.

CHAPTER 3

Getting Started

So far this book has served to show some of the scope of homoeopathy in animal disease and to encourage its use by both veterinary surgeon and pet owner. It is possible, also, that it has left a fear of the unknown, a reluctance to 'get the feet wet' both for vet and owner. This natural hesitation is important for it shows that one has the necessary humility for the difficult task of medicine. Do not succumb to hesitancy but resolve to set out on the path of discovery. Purchase a few remedies (see Appendix 9), or Arnica if one alone is all one dares, and using the following pages get down to business. If, however, more help is needed there are many official bodies, publications, retailers, libraries and advisors to whom one can turn. Their addresses are listed at the back of this book.

The Faculty of Homoeopathy aims to advance the principles and practice of homoeopathy and works in close conjunction with the Homoeopathic Trust for Research and Education and the Royal London Homoeopathic Hospital. These bodies are a source of untiring inspiration, encouragement and help to all professional people. They are central to British homoeopathy and veterinary surgeons should always be ready to consult one or other body. There are regular courses laid on at the Royal London Homoeopathic Hospital and these are an invaluable aid to the veterinary homoeopath as much as to the aspiring doctor for whom they are intended*. The British Association of Homoeopathic Veterinary Surgeons more specifically sets out to help veterinary surgeons in their education and practice and further professional organisations for vets may emerge as members increase. This Association will

---

* *Veterinary courses have been established since the 1st Edition; details from the Faculty of Homoeopathy. (See also p. 28)*

also help in the location of veterinary surgeons who use homoeopathy. The British Homoeopathic Association and the Hahnemann Society are in close liaison with both the professional and the lay populace (that is, those people that are not professionally qualified in one or other field of homoeopathic practice). This wide group obviously includes the ordinary person who wishes to use this form of medicine on his pet. These bodies are a mine of useful information about professional or retail services available, books and self help. They produce many worthwhile publications aimed to guide both the beginner and the established user of homoeopathic remedies and are always ready to answer any queries. The British Homoeopathic Association and the Hahnemann Society publish their own very useful journals.[†]

At the local level there are groups deeply involved in helping one to understand this complex form of medicine. They organise speakers and meetings on all aspects of the subject of homoeopathy. They are a rallying point for those wishing to further the cause of homoeopathy and an invaluable local communication medium; much is to be learnt by attending these groups. Their titles and addresses can be obtained from the National Association of Homoeopathic Groups.

Books on the subject of homoeopathy can be bought or ordered through book shops but the British Homoeopathic Association, Faculty of Homoeopathy and local groups all retail most of the books published. A short bibliography and further reading section is to be found in the Appendix to this book. It is worthwhile stressing again at this point the need for deep and wide reading in order to gain any degree of competence in the practice of veterinary homoeopathy. Much of the available literature may not seem relevant to the veterinary surgeon wishing to deepen his (or her) experience, or the pet owner following his interest in the subject, but be assured that, without the variety of reading to be found amongst the titles mentioned and other books omitted for the sake of conciseness, one's ability to achieve good results in the practice of homoeopathy is sadly

[†] The International Association for Veterinary Homoeopathy (founded in 1986) publishes a Journal twice yearly for veterinary surgeons. (see Appendix 4 & 5)

limited. Each author has tried to pass on his or her own experiences and each reference therefore serves as a means of widening one's own experience. Reference to the treatments in Chapters 8–14 of this book alone or to any other veterinary book alone will only serve to narrow one's sphere of activity and eventually lead to the disillusionment of those who expect to do great things with homoeopathy. Two aspects are of utmost importance when reading. The first is the gathering of homoeopathic principles. Much is written on the human medical side in this field, but sadly the principles of veterinary homoeopathy have been relatively neglected. It is for this reason that this book has devoted a great part of its content to the study of principles alone. Chapters 1–7 are dedicated to the study of the essence and principles of homoeopathy in general and veterinary homoeopathy in particular, without which study one is left as a ship without navigation; how should one proceed and by what route, to arrive at one's required destination?

The second aspect to be considered, when widening one's reading, is the practice of homoeopathy. Again a book such as this is able to supply a great deal of useful information to guide one in the practice of homoeopathic treatment of a wealth of conditions in pets which one can readily recognise. It cannot, however, cover all eventualities. It cannot approach the subject from every direction or give a great number of different slants to the ways of recognising symptoms in animals. For this reason one again arrives at the conclusion that the wider the reading the greater one's flexibility and ability to detect and identify those deviations from the normal which we call illness.

Do not restrict your reading to animal material. Human material is vastly more varied and prolific and is valid to your study within the limitations laid down in Chapter 5. One should I think try to approach the homoeopathic treatment of animals more from a study of totality of symptoms than from a knowledge of diseases and their names and in this I hope the reader will be helped by the pages of this book and by a study of much of the human literature in the Appendix.

Nothing more now remains but to embark upon homoeopathic treatment of animals. I refer you again to Chapter 1, last paragraph, before you start and I would also like to add, at this point, some advice given to my mother before she started using veterinary homoeopathy, and which she subsequently handed on to me:– 'Refer repeatedly to the books on homoeopathic materia medica (and any book which has a section on this subject) and hold in your mind as good a picture as you can of a few important remedies. One day a patient will come into the surgery with a classic case of one of these pictures and you can then use the requisite remedy with an unerring certainty of its applicability (by symptom match) in this case.' The rapid and effective working of the remedy under these ideal conditions is a sure way of boosting your confidence in the ability of homoeopathic remedies to act as they are claimed to act.

It is not the place of this book to advertise manufacturers from who you can obtain your remedies, but addresses are available from the sources of advice to which I have referred in this chapter. Please now resist the temptation to jump to Chapter 8 but read the intervening chapters in order to gain a fuller understanding of how to put your acquired principles into practice.

For those veterinary surgeons who are keen to undertake a fuller study of homoeopathy there is sadly no qualification in veterinary homoeopathy as yet. This situation may be rectified in the future but until then they have no standard by which to judge themselves. It also makes it difficult for the public to know to what depth a veterinary surgeon has studied and used homoeopathy but until such standards exist the problem must remain.‡

‡ *Veterinary surgeons may now study for the 'Vet MF Hom' examination (see footnote p. 25) and obtain a qualification. The British Association of Homoeopathic Veterinary Surgeons will help in the location of those with the qualification or those studying for it.*

CHAPTER 4

Putting Principles into Practice 1: Taking the History in the Veterinary Surgery

Before consulting Chapters 8–14 a word of warning must be issued. This has been said in earlier chapters in a different way but must now be reiterated. Selecting a homoeopathic remedy does not consist entirely of consulting Chapter 8 and perhaps checking in Chapter 17 and leaving it at that. The remedies conveniently placed against those conditions described in Chapters 8–14 are only some of the many remedies which have been found to be of merit in treating such conditions. Some are so likely to be effective in most cases that a note is made to that effect but the majority of the remedies are not the sole recommended treatment. They are simply remedies commonly used in those contexts. If the notes match fairly closely the symptoms presented by the patient the likelihood is that they will work but if the match is not so accurate it is not advisable to 'try it anyway' but more useful to go back to square one.* In this and the next two chapters the logical sequence from square one shall be followed: Taking the history, selecting the remedy, managing the case.

Taking the History

Taking the history of a case is extremely important in homoeopathic veterinary medicine requiring little adaptation on the veterinary surgeon's part. It does however require a modification of attitude and scope. It is the essential basis for choosing a homoeopathic remedy since, in taking an accurate, and hopefully full, history one can present a logical list of symptoms to which to match the remedy. The order is important since it matches the layout of the repertories and materia medica (see book list). It is worthwhile trying to establish a firm routine when taking

See Appendix 8 and p. 37.

your history and it is this which occupies the extra time which a homoeopathic consultation takes as compared with a conventional one.

Introduction to patient
1 a) Observe behaviour in the waiting room
   b) Observe entry to consulting room
      These can tell you so much about the animal and are an opportunity not to be wasted. Note all the points down and refer to No 12 later. In the case of cats the removal from the basket can be a telling time.

The Complaint
2 What is the presenting complaint?
This will be the reason your client has brought the patient in to see you. Note your client's words.
3 Characteristics of each symptom.
Difficult in an animal but still very important. What sort of diarrhoea (character, colour etc.?) What sort of discharge? What type of lesion? etc.
4 The so-called modalities.
What makes the SYMPTOM worse? What makes it better? e.g. weather, temperature, food, drink, rest, motion.
5 Periodicity of complaint.
When is the SYMPTOM worse or when is it better? eg seasons, time of day.
6 Duration of complaint.
How long has it being going on?
7 Circumstances at start.
The client may well say the patient has never been right since, for example, disease, injury, new puppy came into family, owner died, vaccination, etc.
8 Concomitant symptoms.
If sneeze is there a nasal discharge? What sort? If diarrhoea, does the animal strain or not?

The Patient
9 Past medical history.
Previous treatments, vaccinations, other complaints, etc. (One of the many good reasons for communicating with the previous veterinary surgeon in cases of second opinion).
10 Family history if known.
Easier in dog or cat breeding homes than in the average pet's home, although some information may be known.

11 Home environment.
e.g. working dog? Stresses caused by children in family or other pets? Broken home?
12 Mental Symptoms.
a) 'Understanding' type.
Reaction to criticism, consolation, fuss, noise, surrounding activity?
b) 'Will/Manner' type.
Dominant/submissive, aggressive/shy, neat/scruffy, careful/clumsy, impulsive/steady, memory, emotion.
13 General symptoms.
Desires/aversions, physique, posture, gait, sleep, dreams, appetite, thirst, diet, drugs, meals (before/after?), oestrus period (before/after?), effect on PATIENT of geography, season, time, temperature, weather.
14 Particular symptoms.
This is the full examination of the animal. Note, along with symptoms found in each organ system examined, the modalities as per No. 4 <>* with temperature, season, time, weather, moisture, position, etc.

The examination should encompass the entire body in a routine order preferably matched to the text in the materia medica and repertories, viz. Head, Face, Eyes, Ears, Nose, Mouth, Digestive, Urinary, Female/Male, Respiratory, Heart, Circulatory and Blood, Locomotor, Lymphatic System, Nervous System and Skin.

In the examination one must be highly observant using, all the time, one's eyes, ears, nose and touch to ascertain all the details. It is extremely important to give weight to everything the owners say during consultation. Encourage them to discuss anything about the patient however insignificant or foolish it may seem, being careful not to put words in their mouths.

From the history-taking, '*obstacles to recovery*' should come to light. The good veterinarian must seek to eliminate them. They could be nutritional, environmental, historical (qv) or medical. Emotions, drugs, deficiencies, dehydration, mobile fractures, old disease, foreign bodies, vaccination, etc all may represent obstacles.

---

* < *denotes 'worse for'* > *denotes 'better for'*.

CHAPTER 5

Putting Principles into Practice 2: Selecting the Remedy

This chapter deals alone with the actual mechanics of selection. That this chapter is so small a part of the whole, reflects the importance of the principles behind selection, relative to the actual mechanics of selection. For those of you who have jumped straight to this chapter please read no further before you read the earlier part of the book. This sounds to be very imperious advice but is worthwhile since many pitfalls of prescription can be avoided by taking into account the principles discussed in the earlier chapters and introduction. The selection of the remedy ideally suited to the case depends primarily upon the taking of an accurate and full history therefore it will be necessary constantly to refer to Chapter 4 throughout this chapter.

I have repeatedly stated that homoeopathy is the selection of a remedy to match the patient's reaction to disease (that is, the symptoms). What material does one need in order to do this? Referring you again to Hahnemann's words on p. 9, clearly what is needed is:

a) The history or nature of the case. The list of symptoms under logical headings.
b) The nature of the medicines again listed under logical headings similar to those in the history. (See also p. 103).

The first requirement we have just obtained in Chapter 4. The second is contained in Chapter 17 and in the various books on materia medica listed in the Appendix. A guide to where to look in materia medica is given in repertories (books listing symptoms of each part of the body with commonly applicable remedies along side).

A short cut to this process is to use 'ready reckoners' – lists of diseases and suggested remedies worked out by experienced practitioners of the art. These can be found in the human literature and several books on the veterinary side. This book compromises in this respect, containing such a list combined with general considerations of symptoms such as are found in a repertory (Chapter 8). Using such lists will obviously be very much easier than using Hahnemann's first principles, but it cannot lead to such a success rate because no writer can give, in such a list, all conditions affecting choice of remedy under all circumstances of disease. Beware of taking too many short cuts and use ready reckoners only as a guide. (See App. 8 and p. 37).

Hahnemannian Method

Hahnemann's 'Materia Medica Pura' published between 1811 and 1821 contained the provings of 66 remedies. I quote from the 6th edition of the Organon paragraph 153:

'In this search for a homoeopathic specific remedy, that is to say, in the comparison of the collective symptoms of the natural disease with the list of symptoms of known medicines, in order to find among these an artificial morbific agent corresponding by similarity to the disease to be cured, the more striking, singular, uncommon and peculiar (characteristic) signs and symptoms of the case of the disease are chiefly and most solely to be kept in view; for it is more particularly these that very similar ones in the list of symptoms of the selected remedy must correspond to, in order to constitute it the most suitable for effecting the cure. The more general and undefined symptoms:— loss of appetite, headache, debility, restless sleep, discomfort and so forth demand but little attention when of that vague and indefinite character, if they cannot be more accurately described, as symptoms of such a general nature are observed in almost every disease and from almost every drug.'

He also set great store by the mental symptoms displayed in any illness as these most clearly represent the patient's individual response to disease. How difficult it would be with no other guide than the materia medica to match one of 66 remedies to the observed disease. How much more difficult it is now with several thousand from which to choose. Clearly the more one knows by constant reading the easier it is to match remedy to disease but thankfully there are numerous repertories to help.

Repertorising

The basic use of repertories I will illustrate by reference to 'Kents Repertory with Word Index'. Under the headings of the different parts of the body he has listed symptoms with their modalities. Against these he has put names of remedies found to possess these same properties. Those remedies most commonly or strongly possessing these symptoms are in heavy black type, those less so in italics and those least frequently or least strongly in ordinary type. To take a symptom such as 'EYE, SYMPTOMS FROM INJURY' (Kent p244):

Black letters: **Symphytum.**
Italics: *Arnica, Euphrasia, Ledum, Staphysagria*
Ordinary type: Aconite, Calcarea carb., Calcarea sulph, Hamamelis, Silica, Sulphur, Sulph. acid.

From this information one would be very confident prescribing Symphytum if no further homework were done. However, if one looks in Kent under 'EYE, OPACITY FROM WOUNDS' (Kent p. 247) one finds *Euphrasia* in italics. If, therefore, one looks into each symptom one gets a more accurate matching. The more symptoms found and looked up, the more accurate the match. This method has even lent itself to computerisation in the present day, which is a very impersonal, unattractive way to choose a remedy but possibly very effective. It is not possible to hold all the remedies in one's mind, but one can, however, remember numerous keynotes of remedies and these can serve to give immediate reference to a correct remedy in many cases. It is important to remember Hahnemann's words on p. 33, where he extols the virtues of peculiar symptoms by which to choose remedies. One should also recall the tremendous success Hahnemann and his disciples had with only 60 remedies and not be too ready to rush to new and exciting minor remedies. Those most commonly used are such because they fit, most often, the symptoms of most conditions found.

In the veterinary application of Hahnemann's work and the work of repertory compilers we have to consider the likelihood that remedies might not always closely follow symptoms shown in humans when applied to animals. That is the first obstacle to the veterinary use of homoeopathy. As an illustration I cite the often excitatory effect of morphine derivatives in cats compared with no such effect in dogs, only the opposite occurring. One must, therefore, carefully study comparative toxicology and comparative pharmacology to best select remedies of use in different species.

The second great obstacle in homoeopathic prescribing for animals and probably even greater than the first is the lack of mental symptoms gleaned from the patients in the history taking. These mental effects are ranked among Hahnemann's, and more especially his successors', most important pointers to prescribing. One can, however, discern the most obvious ones in some cases and they can prove very useful. I take for example, grief at the loss of a mate or owner, sexual frustration, anxiety, mental shock, fear, anger and sometimes even resentment at, for example, displacement from owner's affections by a new puppy.

The third great obstacle, caused by a limited ability to communicate with animals, is the lack of symptoms of 'sensation' (subjective symptoms) that one can ascertain. For example is an arthritic pain tearing, burning, pulsating? Is an itch crawling, painful, biting, burning? These symptoms are obviously to be ranked among Hahnemann's symptoms peculiar to the disease and therefore of great importance in selecting a remedy. For instance, in the human case, I quote Kent's Repertory showing how such subjective symptoms affect choice of remedy: (p. 1081)
PAIN, FOOT, LIKE NAILS UNDER THE SKIN – Rhus tox,
PAIN, FOOT, PULSATING – Natrum carb.

Clearly there is no hope of attaining this level of prescribing and therefore veterinary homoeopaths must lose a lot of potential curative effect. Homoeopathy in animals would be more widespread if such obstacles were not in the way. For instance Kent lists 19 remedies useful in car sickness.* How is one best to choose between them? The remedies in Chapter 8 are the result of my attempts, and those of others, to select most commonly effective remedies from the many available, but the extent of possible

* *Kent p. 509.*

deviation from that list (leading to failure of the suggested remedies) should now be clear.

In order to select a remedy for a case, and I firmly believe that a single remedy is the best solution even if not always possible, one should decide at what level or levels to operate according to the relative chance of success. The possible levels of treatment are:

a) TREAT THE ROOT CAUSE or rather the inevitable *pathology* arising from that root cause. A good example of an indication to choose this level of treatment is the case of road traffic injury where one would immediately use Arnica (because one can predict the pathology) whatever other symptoms one may wish to treat either simultaneously or more usually subsequently. In the case of shock also, from whatever cause, one would leap to Aconite.

b) TREAT ACCORDING TO THE MENTAL SYMP-TOMS. Where these are clearly discernible as mentioned on p. 35, it is a good idea to treat these first. They are very powerful movers in the cause of disease. (See also Chapter 12.)

c) TREAT ACCORDING TO THE PRESENTING SYMPTOM. This is most commonly, but not always most effectively, the choice in cases coming into the veterinary surgery. In this method of prescribing one uses the presenting sign as a cornerstone made more precise by use of the modalities (see Chapter 9 and 17) and, very importantly, concomitant symptoms. The symptoms found in the case history, recorded under particulars will provide a useful cross reference to choose between remedies. Try to avoid relying too heavily on this method since it may end up only palliative in effect. It is only really useful in cases of simple, acute disease.

d) TREAT PREVIOUS UNDERLYING DISEASE (HISTORICAL). If a patient has experienced in the past (no matter how long ago) an over-ridingly powerful disease influence such that the effects have never left completely, then it can sometimes be of no use to treat what you see, without first treating the previous disease. In this case the remedy to be selected is chosen as if the disease were still present at the time of examination (see

Chapter 10, 11, 12, 14). This principle can even apply when such diseases have occurred in the dam, especially if it was during the pregnancy which gave birth to this patient. (See Eugenics.)

e) TREAT AT THE SO-CALLED CONSTITUTION-AL LEVEL. This is a post Hahnemann concept embodying the philosophy that most human individuals (and this can definitely be applied to animals depending upon one's aptitude to ascertain it) fall into distinct types matched by a particular remedy usually from the list of very deep and wide acting remedies called the 'poly-crests'. This typing is according to the programmed (hereditary, congenital or acquired) response to disease influence. If an animal clearly fits a 'type' portrayed under the description of remedies in materia medica then application of this remedy will act upon the whole patient and produce a favourable tendency towards cure of ALL ailments experienced. It may not produce a full cure in many cases but favourably affect the patient's response to another well-chosen remedy. Chronic disease invariably requires a constitutional remedy. (Care must be taken in use of nosodes for fear of serious aggravation.)

f) SPECIFIC LEVEL (See Chapter 11) and

g) PREVENTIVE LEVEL (See Chapter 14) illustrate homoeopathy and isopathy in use against specific disease entities.

h) FACULTATIVE/REGULATORY/DETOXIFYING prescribing exploits the ability of potentised substances to modify, modulate or regulate the body's absorptive, metabolic and excretory processes with respect to that substance. One can, for example, use potentised Calcium salts to regulate Calcium metabolism or potential toxins to speed elimination of specific toxins.[†]

i) ORGAN SPECIFIC PRESCRIBING utilises the fact that certain remedies have an affinity for certain organs (e.g. Nox vom. for the liver) and can act as a useful adjunct to therapy.

Examples of the above levels of prescribing can be found

---

† *Sulphur and Nux vomica, among other remedies, can serve as 'cleaning' or detoxifying remedies. The French refer to drénage.*

in Chapter 16. Taking all these factors into consideration shows the limitations imposed by strictly adhering to guide lines shown in Chapters 8-14. One must be prepared to deviate from the 'ready reckoner' type of prescribing in order to be reasonably successful.

If a remedy fails to fit very well or if two or three remedies could be chosen, should one try to stick to one remedy, as Hahnemann and many since him maintain, or should one use two or three compatible remedies? One should, at all times, try to find one correct remedy because in this way, when a case is difficult, one is forced to delve deeper into both the patient and the books and this is a useful exercise. If, however, one feels a cure depends upon a rapid selection of a remedy it should do no harm to the case to use two or three remedies. All one loses is the depth and power of the single remedy and the knowledge of which remedy worked so an opportunity for experience is lost. (There is a further hazard of incompatability of remedies but this is difficult to evaluate.)* A further discussion of this occurs in the next chapter in relation to potency. One cannot, in the end, rule out the part played by intuition (part of our valuable sixth sense) in selecting a level of prescribing or choosing the key symptoms upon which to prescribe.

---

*I have been asked many times to put into words my ideas on combination of different levels of prescribing. In order to achieve rapid results I combine on occasions, say the 'Constitutional' approach with, say, the 'presenting symptom' approach. This can have the added advantage, if the patient is able to respond, of stimulating the vital force in more than one direction. This would not be justifiable in Hahnemannian terms but does produce some very interesting results. One can use more than two levels at once. I have presented a schematic approach to this problem in my new book 'Guide to the Homoeopathic Treatment of Beef and Dairy Cattle' in Chapter 5. In summary, however, I believe overuse of multiple remedies will result in a 'confused' case and may even so distort the vital force as to amount to a dangerous procedure (See p. 37, 46, 138/139).

CHAPTER 6

Putting Principles into Practice 3: Managing the Case*

Having decided upon the level of treatment to be employed and chosen carefully that remedy which will best serve the case, there are still further decisions to be made:

By what route should the remedy be applied?

What physical form of the remedy should be used?

What potency should be selected?

What frequency of dosing should be used?

For how long should the dose be given?

When should the effect be checked?

How should the effect of a correct remedy/close remedy/ wrong remedy/ wrong potency be assessed?

I think it is worth discussing all these questions at length, although this does not mean I am claiming any great knowledge on these difficult points.

Route of Administration

The choice must be tailored to suit the conditions to be treated. For example where the whole system is affected by the condition or the condition is caused by an internal derangement then, because the whole body is involved, the whole body must be treated. In this instance, go for an oral or parenteral treatment (that is by mouth or injection) to achieve the desired effect. The condition may, at the same time, demand a topical treatment of superficial lesions. Where a lesion is considered to be purely of local significance e.g. an abrasion or cut, topical treatment may be all

---

* See also p. 103.

that is required but sometimes oral treatment in addition may be beneficial. Injections are more often used in the farm application than in the small animal surgery for the reason that it is not easily practical to give a cow pills several times daily. A very good thing about homoeopathic treatment in the surgery is that effective therapy can be achieved without the need for injections. Water medication is very useful in the large animal context and in the cage-bird or cage-pet situation (see Chapter 11).

Physical Form of Remedy

The choice of form of preparation in which a remedy is prescribed is in part personal and in part governed by the same considerations as above. Pillules, tablets and powders are ideal for oral administration, although my personal preference is for pillules. Lotions, tinctures, creams and ointments are ideal for the topical situation. Tinctures are ideal for water administration but pills will also serve if a tincture in a required remedy is not available. Tinctures can be used orally undiluted but must always be diluted before topical use, especially on tender surfaces e.g. eyes, mucous membranes or sores and wounds. Two or three drops in an eggcupful of water is sufficient strength for application.

Potency

Whenever the subject of potency is raised some people get excited and some get frightened. The tendency is to have very fixed opinions on the subject or to be totally overawed by it. I hope this section will help to unravel some of the mysteries. It would appear to be agreed by most that as the potency increases so does the depth and duration of action. What is lost in this process is breadth of action. High potencies are considered for the purpose of this text to be above 12c, low potencies below 6c. 6c to 12c seems to be a watershed (see p. 11 and Appendix 3).

If one is sure of a remedy for a case one can confidently use a high potency and be sure of its effect. If one is not so sure of the remedy the potency should be kept lower, giving a wider spread of action (see figs. 2–6)

A fertile imagination is needed to gain a graphic concept of the workings of a homoeopathic remedy against disease. Firstly assume there is a curative 'window' through which the remedy must pass to effect a cure. Imagine then a disease entity with several symptom sites (□) and a disease centre: (✕):

Figs. 2 and 3

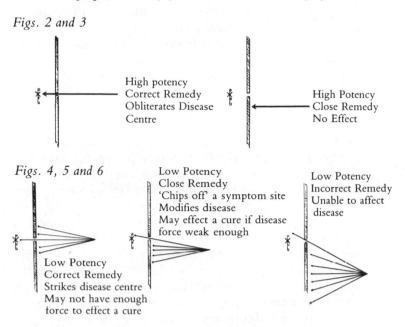

High potency
Correct Remedy
Obliterates Disease
Centre

High Potency
Close Remedy
No Effect

Figs. 4, 5 and 6

Low Potency
Close Remedy
'Chips off' a symptom site
Modifies disease
May effect a cure if disease
force weak enough

Low Potency
Incorrect Remedy
Unable to affect
disease

Low Potency
Correct Remedy
Strikes disease centre
May not have enough
force to effect a cure

The next step when choosing a potency is to consider the patient itself and its disease.* (see footnote p. 46)

a) Is it a chronic disease?
b) Is it an acute dramatic disease?
c) Is it an acute milder disease?
d) Is it the result of a particular agency e.g. trauma?
e) Could a constitutional remedy be used?
f) Is the condition brought about by an overriding mental condition?
g) Is the patient still suffering the effects of a previous illness?

Running through these questions in order:

a) A chronic disease by definition has been about a long time and gone deep and will most likely take a while to recede. If sure of the remedy a high potency is valuable in order to obtain the depth of cure required. I use 30c and above. Often I have found the need to increase potency after a short period on 30 since the effectiveness seems to wane in some cases, probably as a result of all the usefulness of that potency having been utilised.

b) An acute and dramatic disease will brook no delay in activity. Unless absolutely certain of a remedy use 6c or lower in order to benefit from breadth of action. Two remedies together sometimes is an admission of defeat in pure prescribing terms but can nevertheless ensure results which after all is what one is seeking to achieve. If more than one remedy is prescribed they should not be given at the same time; allow at least a five minute interval between.

c) An acute milder disease requires no such haste and urgency. Potency is probably not a great worry here since a failure from using a close remedy in a high potency will not cause a loss of life.

d) If the patient is suffering the results of, for instance, a particular trauma the appropriate remedy in a high potency is certainly advisable if the effects are deep (e.g. shock effects). Here again it is necessary to be sure of the applicability of the remedy. Lower potencies in less severe, less deep acting trauma are probably advisable.

e) If a constitutional remedy is used one is presumably sure of that remedy or the indication for the remedy would not have been felt. Since the animal's constitution is deep go for high potency.

f) In the case of mental conditions (e.g. bereavement) higher potencies are a good idea but one needs to be sure of the remedy otherwise go for low.

g) If a previous illness is suspected of still causing trouble it must be eliminated by a deep acting remedy, that is, in a high potency (see p. 11).

In all cases, if a remedy is needed rapidly and you have it on the shelf, even if only in the potency least suited in your opinion to the case, use the potency you have to hand. That must be better than not using it at all. It must however be remembered that some remedies have a different effect according to potency, that is they are regulatory in their effect. Some examples are:

Hepar sulph.   – low potency provokes suppuration,
              – high potency aborts suppuration.

Merc. sol.   – Similarly
Folliculinum   – low potency arouses female activity,
               – 7c regulates female activity,
               – 12c and above restrains female activity.
Urtica Urens – low potency depresses milk flow,
               – high potency stimulates milk flow.
Salvia   – low potency reduces perspiration,
               – high potency stimulates perspiration.

Frequency

Hahnemann always suggested not giving a second dose until the first had worn off. In the case of easily measurable responses this principle should be followed. Chronic diseases demand a less frequent repetition than acute conditions where, in really acute severe cases, doses can even be given every ten minutes; this is true even in the higher potencies. Once the effect is observed doses can be given according to effect. In chronic conditions administration once or twice daily for a few days and then waiting until an effect is noticed seems a very useful guideline. (See also prevention of disease, Chapter 14.)

Duration

The dose of a confidently selected remedy should be kept up until the effect is seen. After this one doses to effect, the intervals sometimes becoming so long as to constitute a cessation of treatment. The answer to the question 'how long?' is therefore unanswerable in specific time units. Treatment for chronic conditions can be expected to go on for weeks or even months in extreme cases but acute conditions should demand no more than two or three days in the main.

Follow up Visits

How soon should a case be checked for response? A veterinary surgeon has to decide at what interval he should ask to see the patient again. The main reason to see the patient again is to assess effectiveness of the remedy therefore there is again the distinction between acute and chronic conditions. As a rough guide it seems practical to say that acute severe cases should report on the same day, acute milder diseases should report on the following day but chronic diseases, according to the expected progress rate, at one or two weekly intervals.

Assessment

When a patient returns to the surgery an assessment of progress must be made in order to ascertain whether, at the first attempt:*

the correct remedy at the correct potency was chosen,
the correct remedy but wrong potency was chosen,
a close remedy was chosen,
the wrong frequency was chosen,
the wrong duration was decided upon

   After the chosen interval on a correct remedy at the correct potency one can see:
a) In the case of a chronic condition, with or without an improvement in the disease, a distinct improvement in the well being of the patient as a whole can be seen. Continue treatment, according to frequency and duration principles, (p. 43).
b) In the case of a chronic condition a failure to alter the presenting complaint along with a disturbing recurrence of a previous complaint (recapitulation of the earlier stages of chronic disease) which may at the time have been considered unrelated to the present complaint. Continue treatment as above.
c) The cure can, again in a chronic condition, work from within outwards so that deeper troubles (e.g. heart, digestive, mental) clear up before a skin complaint. Continue treatment as above.
d) A complete cure or good progress along that route can occur in a very short time. Only continue treatment if necessary.
e) It is possible to have selected correctly and fail to achieve any result whatsoever. In this case it is possible that one

---

* *For the purpose of this section I am assuming no conventional drug (suppressive) factors are present. These can lead to even greater complexities as the effects wear off on stopping intake of drugs.*

has missed, in the earlier history taking, the significance of an overriding effect by an earlier disease not completely cured. Canine Parvovirus or Feline Enteritis, Leptospiral Jaundice, difficult pregnancy, various mental considerations can all (with many other conditions) leave their mark. The correct nosode or similium should be applied without delay [see p. 118 et seq and p. 36 (d)].

There are several indications of a correct remedy in the wrong potency having been chosen:

a) An apparent worsening of the disease (aggravation). The treatment should be discontinued forthwith to test if this is the case. If so the effect will be temporary. Continue treatment later with a higher potency if the condition is not cured.

b) Inadequate depth of effect will indicate a remedy in too low a potency.

c) Rarely, a local pathological condition will fail to respond to too high a potency where it seems that the remedy runs on too high a plane for the disease presented. It can be analogous to shooting over the enemy's head. If sure of the remedy, lower the potency.

An incorrect remedy that is very close can produce a change in symptoms (see figs 2-6, p. 41) if the potency is low enough. Go back to square one and take account of the new symptoms in order to choose the correct remedy. Often it is a closely related remedy such as prescribed Mercurius cor. needing, instead, Mercurius sol.

A wrong remedy produces no effect if it is not close enough or not in low enough potency (see figs 2-6, p. 41). Go back to the history taking time to find the error in prescribing, remembering especially the adverse influence of previous disease, which has been suppressed, against an apparently correct remedy (see p. 36 (d)).

Rarely a remedy can be correct and then fail. A second remedy can then be needed and eventually an alternation of the two can be required. Rhus tox. and Bryonia commonly show this alternating relationship where the modalities of a rheumatic condition alternate between those of these two remedies.

If doses are given too frequently or for too long a great confusion can arise. At first the case may improve but then it can relapse to varying degrees. This can be a result of having carried out a proving (that is producing the symptoms of the remedy as did Hahnemann in his very first tests). The confusion then confronting the prescriber is:

a) Is the remedy wrong; the change in the disease being a coincidental improvement then relapse?
b) Is a correct remedy prescribed wrongly, so producing a proving?

To unravel this, all one can do is cease treatment immediately and observe results. Usually it is a proving and the symptoms will immediately subside. I think it is important that no prescription should be refilled without the knowledge of the prescribing veterinary surgeon, to prevent unwitting over treatment[†] (See also pp. 37/38, 137/138).

Whereas it is often said that there are no side effects of homoeopathic treatment some of the aforementioned sequelae could be misread as such. They are clearly not side effects in the true sense of the word but merely extraneous effects of the primary purpose nor do they last. An open mind is essential not only before prescribing but, as the foregoing points demonstrate, after prescribing too. The sequelae of the treatment must be read with care and acted upon correctly in order to achieve the deep and lasting cure for which one strives.

[†] We are not discussing here the amount given at any one time. This factor appears to be unimportant. As long as the organism is *introduced* to the potentised remedy there is no need to worry about body size, etc. The dose appears to be energetic in nature and therefore not dependent upon quantity given.

[*] *from page 41* If the vital force is seriously disabled by severe chronic disease, beware of high potencies.

CHAPTER 7

Putting Principles into Practice 4: Care of the Remedies

Very little is understood of the real nature of homoeopathic remedies in potency. There is still no accepted reliable method of measuring their quality and this reason alone is enough to suggest that it is sensible only to acquire them from reputable sources. Having acquired them it is of major importance to look after them very carefully to ensure that their efficacy is not lost during their potentially very long life. This applies as well to their storage in a veterinary surgery as in the home.

The nature of the remedy appears to be a form of energy pattern harnessed from the original substance during the potentising process. Thus, although all conventionally measurable traces of the original substance are lost, and with them the power to produce side effects, the curative power is enhanced and trapped in what must be a fairly labile form.

It is not necessary to go to the lengths of air-conditioned storage, special containers and so forth but it is essential to be reasonably careful to choose a storage place for them which allows them to remain in a fairly constant environment. This environment wants to be free from excessive damp, cold or heat, free from direct sunlight and clear of all very strong smelling substances.

Camphor preparations, in homoeopathic potency or mother tinctures, should be stored separately. The container should be glass but although there is talk of long term damage to a remedy by storage in plastic there appears to be no short-term deleterious effect. Permeable products such as paper or cardboard should not be used since they are too subject to influence from the environment.

The pills should not be handled except when actually administering the remedy to the patient, any pills that have been handled should not be returned to the bottle. Pills may conveniently be dispensed into the bottle cap prior to dosing and, if the patient allows, be tossed from the cap directly into the mouth. The bottles of two remedies should not be opened at the same time, and there should be at least a five minute interval between giving doses of different remedies. The remedies should not be given with food.

One day much of this book may be rendered obsolete and especially this chapter, as research (actively proceeding at present) unfolds more of the nature of remedies and their mode of action. Many beliefs passed on in these pages may seem strange when it is known what 'potency' is and it can be measured. Then it will be possible to ascertain exactly what does and does not affect it. Until that day, however, I think it is important to adhere to the above advice in order to ensure the efficacy of purchased remedies.

CHAPTER 8

Symptoms of Disease with some Recommended Treatments

This chapter is designed on the basic layout of Kent's Repertory for the body systems and should fit well with the history taking (Particulars section) see Chapter 4. Symptoms of the mind (Mentals), appearing first in most repertories as a very important prescribing factor in human medicine, will be dealt with on their own later (Chapter 12), since there has not yet been devised a way of giving it priority in all cases of animal disease. I must reiterate that this chapter should not be used as a 'bible' of veterinary homoeopathy in small animals but as a guide in methodology and as an insight into some very useful remedies. Please do be sure to read a wider selection of books than this one alone (see bibliography). Please also be encouraged to read the chapters on principles before using this chapter. The use of these remedies is bound to be more successful if a wider understanding of homoeopathy is attained prior to attempting its practice. Please also adhere to good nursing and dietary principles (additional notes p. 103)

The symptoms to be discussed will appear under the following headings in the order given:

Head and Face, Eyes, Ears, Nose, Mouth, Digestive System, Urinary System, Male Sexual System, Female Sexual System (including Breeding), Respiratory System, Heart, Circulatory and Blood System, Lymphatic System, Locomotor System, Skin, Nervous System, Endocrines.

Some variation is shown from Kent and Boericke for which I make no apology. The needs of the veterinary surgeon are different from those of the doctor. I suggest that the notes from the clinical examination follow the above order for convenience.

Many apparent opportunities for expansion, inclusion of further symptoms and remedies etc., will appear to the observant reader but I felt that, in compiling this chapter, too full a discussion would lead to loss of clarity and direction. It is not intended to be a total veterinary manual. A greater attempt in this direction could be made in a future volume on all species. If no mention is made of species please assume the comments apply to all species. Exceptions will be highlighted. Serious conditions require veterinary help.

When a remedy is given under a particular disease or symptom it is very likely to be useful if one can match the properties of the remedy shown in Chapter 17 with other concomitant symptoms in the patient. Remedies fitting the generalities of the case can always be used if indicated in addition to those described (see p. 37). Constitutional prescribing is of especial importance in chronic disease.

Head and Face

One must distinguish between disease of the bones of head and face and disease of the accompanying soft tissues (muscles, skin, etc.). For diseases of injury refer to appropriate sections on this subject (p. 111). For injury to the brain and disease of the brain see Nervous System.

Pathology Encountered in the Head and Facial Area

a) BONY LUMPS (Exostoses) or DEFORMITIES:

These can occur anywhere on the head for unknown reasons or as a result of previous injury. Remedies powerfully effective in this field are:
Forehead, upper jaw and nasal area   – Aurum met.,
Lower jaw with degenerative changes– Calc. fluor. too
Especially lower jaw with lymph nodes– Hekla lava. swollen (Can include Cranium and upper jaw)

This latter pattern is seen especially in Craniomandibular Osteopathy in the West Highland White Terrier. Also of use in this condition are Pituitary Extracts or Thyroid in potency.

With tooth involvement especially up- – Mercurius
per jaw and under eyes, putrid breath,   sol.
profuse saliva, facial deformity, swollen lymph nodes and contracture of
masticatory muscles

The picture of **Malar abscess** fits this general picture
wherein the conventional course of action is extraction
of the offending tooth. Homoeopathy is still a very
useful adjunct to this treatment.

Swelling and necrosis of the jaw bone – Phosphorus,
with puffy eyelids etc.
Discrete swelling on (especially) lower – Kali iod.,
jaw
Swelling and atrophy of turbinates – Lemma
with consequent distortion of the nose   minor.
in young animals

b) SOFT TISSUES:

Allergy shows frequently in the facial area as an
urticarial swelling of the eyelids, and possibly entire
face. Apart from ascertaining the cause if possible, treat
according to symptoms (with Galphimia glauca as a
general antiallergic remedy).

With irritation   – Urtica urens.
Oedema and pain   – Apis mel.
Upper eyelids especially   – Kali carb.
Cheeks, lips, crusted eyes, stopped up – Bovista.
nose
Swollen upper and lower eyelids   – Phosphorus.

These remedies are only suggestions with general
guiding symptoms provided. See also Conjunctivitis (p.
53) and Eyelids (p. 54). Generally this problem is seen in
dogs but cats can sometimes show it especially in
reaction to an antibiotic.
Cellulitis in a cat's face following a cat bite should not
be confused with this condition (use Hepar Sulph.).
Where incomplete abscessation or recurring suppuration from an old wound occurs use Silicea.
Myositis (inflammation of the muscle) generally only
occurs in one specific condition of unknown aetiology

but injury may be involved – Temporal Myositis (also called Eosinophilic Myositis or Atrophic Myositis). It is usually seen in large breeds of dog. The muscles over the head and around the throat become inflamed, painful and swollen and in more advanced cases shrink (contracture). Eating and swallowing become increasingly difficult and the patient may become vicious as a result of pain and distress. Voice change, locked jaw and changed facial expression can occur (cf. Tetanus). This picture is beautifully matched by Cedron. As a nerve may be involved cure is not necessarily assured. Nursing assumes vital importance. Other remedies which can be of use are: Aconite, Arnica, Gelsemium and Hypericum. Use Merurius sol. where contracture is noticeable. Kali iod, may also be of use.

Opisthotonus is a symptom in which the head is drawn back along the neck and shoulders. The forelimbs are usually extended see Tetanus p. 118 and Nervous System p. 110.

Furunculosis affects the nose area, chin and upper jaw mostly. There is usually a deep infection with Staphylococcus and often follicular mange. Use: Staphylococcus nosode, Silicea, Hepar Sulph. and topical mange treatment (see also Skin p. 96 and Eyelids p. 54).

Rodent Ulcer see Mouth and Skin.

Eyes

Eye conditions constitute one of the great spheres of action of homoeopathy. Conventional medicine finds the eyes difficult to treat but careful selection of the correct homoeopathic remedy can achieve amazing results. Treatment of eyes is best left to the veterinary surgeon since close examination of the eye is essential and consequences of failure are serious.

Disorders of Eye Movement are dealt with under Nervous System p. 100.

All superficial inflammation of the eye and eye area can be helped by Calendula lotion, or tincture diluted. Also Euphrasia eye lotion is a very useful preparation where symptoms indicate.

Injury to eye and eye area is dealt with under Injury p. 111. Check for foreign body.

Conjunctivitis. A great number of remedies act on the conjunctiva but only the most useful ones will be discussed here:

Intensely red or pink conjunctiva profuse mucopurulent discharge, granular conjunctivitis, with or without clouding of the cornea and photophobia (abdominal symptoms may accompany)	Argent nit.
Conjunctivitis acquired by travelling with head out of car window aggravated by cold, dry wind, eyes water profusely and patient rubs them	Euphrasia
Profuse lachrymation, dilated pupils, photophobia also aggravated by cold winds	Aconite.
After removal of foreign bodies or after operations	Aconite.
Worse at night and worse for heat	Sulphur.
Agglutination, photophobia, burning corrosive tears, eyes dull and sunken	Arsen alb.
Bland tears, sensitive to light	Allium cepa.
Sensitive to light, comes and goes, creamy pus, desire to rub, worse for wind	Pulsatilla.
With photophobia, cloudy cornea, especially older dog, yellow sclera, no inflammation	Conium mac.
Lids red and inflamed, burning discharges, leaving white flakes	Sanicula.
Granular, purulent, spreads down face	Jequirity. (Arbrus precatorius)
Watery and itchy, worse in open air and after exercise	Sabadilla.
With sore cheeks, itchiness, agglutination, dilated pupil, suppuration	Ledum.
Photophobia, very injected sclera, corneal ulcer, blepharospasm	Merc. sol.
Worse photophobia, very constricted pupil	Merc. cor.

Red margins of lids, inflammation from– Calc. carb.
foreign body, cold air aggravates, quiver-
ing lids, dilated pupils, morning agglu-
tination
Spasm of lids, red, corrosive tears, usually– Natrum mur.
lateral canthus
Not affected by light, insensible, cloudy – Lycopodium.
Photophobia, rubbing, profuse lachryma– Cobaltum.
tion, nose waters
From entropion or trichiasis   – Borax.
Photophobia,   enlarged   meibomian– Rhus tox.
glands, purulent
Ropy pus, yellowish, itching oedema, no– Kali bich.
pain or photophobia

Nosodes of Distemper or Cat Flu, if these viruses are
involved, can prove very useful (or even vital) adjuncts to
treatment by the appropriate similimum.

Eyelids

Growths. Conventionally these are removed but it is well
worth trying homoeopathic treatment first to try to prevent
this eventuality. Useful remedies are:

Kali iod., Conium (old dog syndrome), Staphisagria (hard
lumps in margins) and especially Thuja.

Inflammation. Primarily consider Rhus tox, if other
mucocutaneous junctions involved consider Nitric acid.
Most of the conjunctivitis remedies can apply here according to the similia principle (use the preceding pages as a
guide). If the lids are red and painful and granulated in
appearance and there is swelling of the face consider
Cinnabaris, see also Furunculosis p. 52.

Entropion. Borax is the prime remedy here and may avert
surgery. It is a long term treatment.

If gross conjuctivitis with blepharospasm– Natrum mur.

Where inflammation of lids has caused swelling leading to
inturned eyelids consider Tellurium.

Fissures in Eyelids. Graphites or Petroleum are indicated
but other skin signs usually guide one to the correct
remedy.

Trichiasis and Dystichiasis (misplaced or extra eyelashes). Borax is worth trying but repeated plucking is also advisable, since they are so able to damage the eye.

Lachrymal Duct and Glands

Meibomian Glands in the margins of the lids can become inflamed. This is almost impossible to distinguish from inflammation of the eyelid and conjunctiva.

The same remedies apply according to
symptoms shown, especially: – Rhus tox.
If intolerance of milk is involved   – Aethusia.

Lachrymal Duct Blockage usually a chronic sequel of Feline viral respiratory infections. Rarely blocked in dogs. May also be sequel of injury.

– Argentum met., Calc. carb., Pulsatilla, Silicea, Symphytum according to symptoms.

Lachrymal Gland Inflamed – Hepar sulph., Iodum (acute), Pulsatilla, Silicea according to symptoms.

Affections of Lachrymal Puncta (opening in lower lid) – Cinnabaris.

If the Lachrymal Gland ceases to function this leads to the serious condition of Keratitis Sicca, 'Dry Eye'. This affects especially West Highland White Terriers and aetiology is not known. False tears are an essential immediate first aid to prevent damage to cornea. To prevent surgery being necessary try Zincum met., Veratrum alb., or Senega (see case history Chapter 16).

The Cornea

This is the bright clear front of the eyeball through which light passes to the lens. Its clarity is upset by any damage or change in the fluid balance system which is maintained by evaporation from the front surface and replenishment from the chamber behind. There are no blood vessels in the normal cornea.

Ulceration, pigmentation, vascularisation, cloudiness, granular appearance and rupture are all possible conditions to be observed. All are able to be successfully resolved if correctly treated homoeopathically and if treatment is started in good time. Management of these conditions represents one of the special wonders of homoeopathy. The eye, despite its fragile appearance, has the most wonderful powers of recovery if correctly encouraged. All forms of surgery of the Cornea should be avoidable if one gets a favourable response to treatment.

Blueing of the Cornea is an occasional side effect of Hepatitis vaccination in the dog, the nosode is useful.

Cloudiness: This can be a sign of inflammation of the Cornea (Keratitis) or a part of a general ageing process.

Keratitis often in conjunction with conjunctivitis, many remedies serve both.

Cloudy, inflamed conjunctiva with purulent discharge	Argentum nit.
Pearly white conjunctiva, some glaucoma (swollen eye from internal pressure)	Phosphorus.
Showing internal ill health, dull eye, fails to respond to light, nose stopped up, fan like movement of nostrils, liver symptoms	Lycopodium.
Chronic dilation of pupils, Cataract, usually fat constitution	Calc. carb.
No pain or photophobia	Kali bich.
Very photophobic	Merc. cor.
With very dilated pupil, some glaucoma	Belladonna.
Cornea like ground glass, opthalmia present, early ulcer, night aggravation	Sulphur.

Opacity:

Usually with Cataract	Calc. fluor.
With Cataract	Causticum.
With purulent conjunctivitis	Argent. nit.
Water all the time, conjunctivitis, blueing	Euphrasia.
With sneezing coryza	Naphthalinum

Cineraria eye lotion is very useful especially after injury (long term treatment). Silicea removes scars after ulceration, injury, surgery etc (long term treatment).

Both cloudiness and opacity can result from Keratitis Sicca

see p. 55 if a result of ageing consider Conium.

Corneal Ulceration: In this condition the outer membrane of the cornea is lost in one area as a result of infection, inflammation or damage. More layers may become affected and eventually rupture is possible (see sequelae).

Purulent discharge, red conjunctiva, closes– Argent nit.
eye, Cornea clouds almost to the point of
being opaque, photophobia in warm room

Anyone who has seen what a 'styptic pencil' can do to the front of the eye will know what Argent nit. can cure.

Indolent ulcer in a fat subject (usually),– Calc. carb.
with or without cataract, usually aged dog
Watery eye, frequent blinking, swollen– Euphrasia.
lids, sticky mucus on cornea. Photophobia, especially in daylight, corneal opacity
or blueness
Swollen lids, ropy mucus, very little pain,– Kali bich.
deep ulceration, conjunctivitis
A truly wonderful remedy in the case of– Merc. cor.
great photophobia, fear of the eye being
touched, no pupil movement, deep ulceration (other mercurial signs are usually
present e.g. thirst with wet mouth, smelly
breath)
A very similar remedy with less photo– Merc. sol.
phobia and more chronicity
Also in cases of great photophobia   – Conium.
In cases where suppurative processes have– Hepar sulph.
started or with pus in the eye itself too
(Hypopion). This occurs especially after
cat claw injuries to the eye

Injury:
Puncture   – Ledum.
Laceration   – Staphisagria.

Sequelae
Perforation giving rise to Keratocoele or Staphyloma (swellings on the front of the eye):
In early stages to reduce swelling   – Apis mel.
To complete healing   – Merc. sol.

Vascularisation and Pigmentation: Merc. sol. is a very effective long term treatment, but early effects are immediately obvious.

If great photophobia	– Aurum met.
Opaque scars: Long term treatment	– Silicea.

Lens

Cataract, is an opacity of the lens, not always possible to clear but Cineraria eye lotion in the long term can help clear the condition. Also use:–

Cloudy lens	– Sulphur.
Aged dog and from injury	– Conium.
Incipient cataract	– Nat. mur.
Fat, indigestion, ageing	– Calc. carb.
Degeneration with age	– Phosphorus.
Degeneration after eye surgery	– Senega.
Dry or opaque, usually sneezing coryza	– Naphthalinum.

Also Silicea 30 as long term treatment can help and consider Calc. Fluor. but do not repeat too often.

Pupil

The pupil of the eye is designed to open and close in response to dark and light respectively. When this fails to happen it is a symptom to be noted. It is either dilated or contracted.

PUPIL DILATED:

    Argent nit.,
★ Belladonna,
    Calc. carb. (ageing),
    Conium (injury or ageing),
    Gelsemium,
    Glonoine (especially useful in heat stroke),
    Hyoscyamus,
    Stramonium,
    Spigelia (Eye, heart, nervous system remedy).

Thus when concomitant symptoms are correct for any of these remedies (or others) they may be used with confidence.

Glaucoma can occur with pupil dilation (see p. 59).

Also remember Symphytum if orbital area is damaged by trauma, Helleborus if concussion.

Key Gaskell Syndrome in cats, a newly discovered syndrome[†], may be helped most satisfactorily in its early stages by Belladonna, Calc. carb., Hyoscyamus, Stramonium or Wyethia (dilated pupils are a major symptom). Gelsemium can also play a part. See separate section on p. 120.

PUPIL CONTRACTED: In cases of **Ophthalmitis** (qv), that is, inflammation of whole eye, contracted pupil can lead to, or is a result of, pain.

Consider:
With nervous cause	– Opium, Phyostigmine.
With Ophthalmitis	– Rhus tox.
Usually with conjunctivitis	– Thuja.

Contracted pupil is a symptom of lead poisoning, use Plumbum met with the similimum. It is important to relieve the poisoning and remove the source.

Again there are a great many more remedies which can help contracted pupils. Concomitant symptoms must be the guide to selection.

Arnica can be used with dilated or contracted pupils, if as a result of injury to brain or head. Similarly Helleborus, although this usually suits a dilated pupil, with eyes turned upwards.

Eyeball

Glaucoma is a condition of the eyeball where the pressure within is so great as to make the eye swell, thus damaging its internal structures including the optic nerve. Since the angle of drainage in the anterior chamber is opened by pupillo-constriction a dilated pupil is not a desirable symptom (see Pupils dilated).

GLAUCOMA remedies:

Early stage of fever	– Aconite.

[†] *At time of 1st edition.*

59

With pupil dilation and other — Belladonna.
concomitant signs
With Ophthalmitis — Phosphorus.

Also Gelsemium and Spigelia. Again select a remedy according to concomitants.

Ophthalmitis, (total deep inflammation of the eye). This is a very painful condition. The pupil is usually constricted in response to the pain which, because of tension in the muscle of the pupil, increases the pain; a vicious circle.

Remedies most likely to help in this condition:

with pupillo constriction, — *Rhus tox.
purulent discharge, rheumatics
With pupil dilation — Belladonna.
— *Phosphorus.
In early stages — Aconite.
If clouding in the eye — Euphrasia.
If blood in the eye — Hamamelis.
With catarrhal inflammation — Kali bich.
If pus present (use high potency) — Hepar sulph.
Redness of whole eye — Cinnabaris.

Quick action is necessary to avoid permanent damage to the sensitive eye structures.
 Use Symphytum if injury to eyeball by blow from a blunt instrument.

Orbital Area. Physical damage to the area is potentially serious and Symphytum seems to have an uncanny effect on any injury caused by a blow from a blunt instrument e.g. dog kicked by a horse. Hamamelis and Arnica are also useful, Hamamelis especially where there is bleeding into the eye. Conium has its special sphere of action affecting surgical injury to this area and the eye.

Other useful remedies are:

Puncture wound to the eye — Ledum
Cellulitis — Rhus tox.
Oedematous swelling — Apis mel.
Growths or periostitis — Kali iod.

A rare sequel to a blow on the head is **detached retina**.

Gelsemium is favoured here although the author has no experience of this. Naphthalinum is also indicated.

Epiphora (overflow of tears) see blocked Lachrymal duct. p. 55 and Influenza p. 119. Also:

Allium cepa, Cobaltum, Euphrasia, Sabadilla.

Everyone has seen the pet who sits too close to the fire. Some have eye complaints stemming from this, consider:

Aconite, Glonoine, *Merc. sol. and Natrum sulph.

Ears

Ears may conveniently be studied in two parts,
1 External ear and ear flap (see also skin).
2 Middle ear/Internal ear,
the most commonly occurring being trouble in the external ear canal. This is commonly but loosely referred to as Canker. Since examination by Auriscope is essential, treatment of the ear is best left to the veterinary surgeon. Precipitating causes must be found and lesions in the ear canal identified to select a remedy.

All the usual procedures for examination and attention to problems eg hair, foreign body, etc must be followed. Discharges and tissue debris can be removed by use of a proprietory natural debriding agent and parasites can eliminated (see Ear Mites). Taking all such veterinary care for granted, homoeopathic treatment alone will be discussed here.

External Ear Canal

Ear Mites. Must be eliminated either by use of proprietory chemicals or herbal insecticides (they are not insects but are susceptible to similar substances). Red/brown wax, with or without pus, usually indicates the presence of ear mites. Psorinum or Sulphur, depending on the nature of discharges, are good homoeopathic remedies given internally to help remove the discharge and to render the environment hostile to mites. They may even serve to eliminate the infection by themselves. Conium is also useful, in this condition.

Foul Discharges, Pus etc. Many of the remedies affecting this condition are the deep acting polycrests which will work better if used at constitutional level of prescribing, but consider especially:

Arsen alb., Arsen iod., Calc carb., Causticum, Graphites, Hepar sulph., Kali bich. (usually swollen ear canal and glands), Kali carb., Kali sulph., Kreosotum, Mercurius (canal inflamed, ulcers), Psorinum, Pulsatilla, Rhus tox. and Sulphur. If fishy discharges, Sanicula or Tellurium.

As usual, characteristic pointers to the remedies should be found.

Inflammation with Discharges

In early stages of inflammation   – Aconite.
If red, hot and swollen   – Belladonna.

Causticum, Conium., Graphites, Kali bich., Mercurius, Rhus tox. and Sulphur are also very useful remedies.

   If severe and sudden in the summer always suspect grass seed. After removal use Calendula lotion or tincture in the canal to ease the pain and promote healing.

Ear Flap

Of less prescribing importance than discharge:

Haematoma   – Arnica, Hamamelis.
Scaly surface, scabby edge   – Tellurium.
Dry, scaly skin   – Arsen. alb.
Dirty, smelly eczema around ear   – Psorinum.
Red, dry, itchy, worse warm room   – Sulphur.

Middle/Inner Ear

Usually manifested as a catarrhal deafness or loss of balance and holding head to one side. There can be eye movement (nystagmus) too. (**Age deafness** is a separate refractory problem but consider Argent met., Causticum, Silicea, and Thiosinaminum). **The loss of balance** (see p. 102) is helped by proper treatment of the external ear and by:

Staggering, trembling and weakness	– Gelsemium.
Falls when shakes head or tends to fall left	– Conium.
Better when lying down	– Cocculus
When moving downwards	– Borax.
Tends to fall forwards	– Bryonia.
Falls to left	– Nat. mur.
Falls to right	– Aconite.
	– Causticum
Circles to the right	– Causticum.
Circles to the left	– Rhus tox.

Catarrhal Deafness. Consider:

Agraphis nutans (especially cats), Borax, Calcarea, Kali mur. and Pulsatilla. according to particular and general symptoms.

The loss of balance as a result of middle or inner ear infection is a good indication for the use of antibiotics to reduce the risk of damage. Homoeopathic remedies should not be relied upon to work fast enough here unless one is totally sure of one's ability.

Nose

Sneezing: ★Check for foreign body. If present or suspected give Silicea unless it is easily retrievable. If not present:

With watery discharge	– Nat. mur., Nux vom.,
	– Sabad.
With blood	– Nitric acid.
With itchy skin, worse with heat	– Sulphur.

Snuffles:

Bland, creamy discharge, can be with blood	– Pulsatilla.
Corrosive discharge, nose blocked but runs	– Arsen. alb.
Worse for warm room, worse at night	– Nux vomica.
Chronic	– Calc carb., Silicea.

Blocked Nose: — Silicea.
Crusty blocked nose — Teucrum mar.
No discharge, but blocked up, — Sticta. pulm.
voice altered
With bleeding — Ipecac.
Worse for wet, cold weather — Rhus tox.
Yellow/Green thick discharge — Calc. fluor.
Yellow ropy catarrh — Kali bich.
With Haemorrhage — Ferrum phos,
Phosphorus.

Cat Flu: Is the specific nasal disease to consider in this section. Treat by nosode and relevant similium and ensure that patient is not dehydrated through lack of water intake (see Chapter 11).

Debility afterwards, help build up with:

China, Ferrum phos. or Phos. acid.

Cracked Skin:
e.g. post Distemper — Nitric acid.

Nose Bleeds (Epistaxis):

General remedy — Hamamelis.
Sudden — Phosphorus.
With sneeze — Carbo veg., Nitric acid.
Especially if injury — Arnica.
Blocked/Bleeding — Ipecac.
With vomiting — Eupatorium
perfoliatum.

Sores at edges of nostrils — Nitric acid.

Loss of Pigmentation (dogs especially).
No definitely indicated remedy. Try the trace elements:

Cobaltum, Cuprum, Ferrum, Manganum and Zincum.

This is a condition of no medical importance but does disfigure an animal from the show point of view. Seaweed preparations have also been tried with varying results.

Sinuses: are functionally a part of the nasal system and all conditions of these are as for nasal symptoms.

Mouth

Since the mouth is the opening of the alimentary canal and the respiratory system, it shares a common involvement with disease of the alimentary system and can show symptoms from the respiratory system. However it is entirely visible and therefore is a key area for picking up signs of disease.

Smell from the Mouth: This can originate from kidney disease, bad teeth, intestinal worms, ketosis, neoplastic conditions, throat disease, digestive disorder or mouth disease itself. As such therefore it is not useful in itself but only in the context of the whole animal.

Ulcerated Mouth: Where such ulcers are around the borders of mouth and skin, that is, on edge of lips consider Nitric acid.

Rodent Ulcer is to be found around the mouth and Cistus can, Conium, Mercurius and Nitric acid have all been found to be helpful (see also Skin) Gallium aparine Ø is of use topically and Calendula lotion. There also appears to be a hormonal link here as in miliary eczema and therefore one should consider. (See also p. 99 and p. 147)

Testosterone potentised, Agnus castus and Ustilago maydis.

Ulcers on tongue, palate, gums and inside cheeks. Consider:

Thirst, profuse saliva, sometimes vomiting and diarrhoea, puffy gums, sometimes with bleeding from gums, Uraemic ulcers	– Mercurials.
Blood from gums	– Phosphorus.
Kidney disease and Uraemic ulcers	– Kali chlor.
Slimy mouth	– Hydrastis.
Vesicles becoming usually well circumscribed ulcers	– Borax.

Other remedies – Arum triphyllum and Nitric acid.

Profuse Salivation: When an animal shows profuse salivation it is a result of overproduction or failure to swallow. Consider in the latter case therefore, **sore**

throats: Baryta carb. (especially if the Lymph glands are swollen in the neck), Causticum, Hepar sulph., Merc cyanatus, Merc sol., Phytolacca and Silicea. (See also p. 89)

Also consider:

Obstructed Throat – take appropriate action.

Tetanus (see also p. 118). Seek immediate veterinary attention.

Foreign Body in Mouth e.g. stick across the teeth – take appropriate action.

In the case of **Overproduction** of Saliva consider:

Baptisia, Lyssin, Mercurial remedies, Pilocarpine and Pulsatilla.

Travel Sickness can present as drooling saliva (see p. 72)

Can also be caused by disagreeable taste or fastidious appetite (especially cats), this is not pathological.

Underproduction of Saliva: Leads to a dry mouth. This is seen primarily in dehydration (rehydration therapy from your veterinary surgeon is essential) and in Key Gaskell Syndrome cats (see p. 120). Shock can also lead to a dry mouth, Aconite and Arnica may be helpful here. Where there is a dry mouth in association with other illness consider Apis mel., Arsen alb., Belladonna or Lycopodium.

Sore Throats with dry mouths (as opposed to profuse salivation from sore throat on p. 65) lead one to think of:

Hot, painful, shiny throat upset by noise or movement, red eyes	– Belladonna.
Constantly seeks fresh air, throat is grossly swollen and oedematous	– Apis mel.
Dry mouth, with absence of thirst	– Pulsatilla.
Dry mouth with large thirst	– Arsen alb.

Gums can show ulceration (as for the mouth) and disease associated with the teeth – (see p. 67). Remedies: Apis, Mercurius, Phosphorus, Arsenicum, Kreosotum, Nitric Acid, Chamomilla. (See also p. 140).

There is also the condition known as **Epulis**, consider here Calc. carb., Calc. fluor. or Thuja.

Teeth

Tartar on the teeth leads to a foul mouth, receding gums, loose teeth, dental abscesses,[†] ulceration and pain. The teeth should be properly attended to by a veterinary surgeon, loose and diseased teeth being extracted and tartar removed. Arnica should be given before, during and after this operation. Calendula lotion should be used to soothe the sores and reduce the inflammation. Fragaria should be given to help prevent new tartar build-up, a few doses given every two months will help. Little carbohydrate should be given in the diet and a mouthwash should be used to clean the teeth regularly. There are homoeopathic/herbal mouthwashes available. Mercurial remedies will aid recovery if there is much saliva and swollen gums.

In young dogs **'Teething'** can be a problem. Here the remedy of choice is Chamomilla for all ills stemming from this teething state. Teething problems can affect any or all of the entire body system including the mental sphere. Malicious chewing of furniture, etc. at this stage can be helped in some cases by Chamomilla.

Delayed Dentition, consider Calc. carb. or Calc. phos. Where there are defects in the enamel at this stage consider Calc. fluor. or Fluoric acid.

The Digestive System

The digestive system comprises the Oesophagus, Stomach, Intestines, Anus, Liver, Pancreas and the Mouth (already discussed). Vomiting and Diarrhoea will also be included in this section.

Oesophagus

Dilated: This condition is seen in some young puppies and in Key Gaskell Syndrome (p. 120) in cats. Consider:

[†] *Malar Abscess see p. 51.*

Alumina, Arsen alb., Plumbum, Stramonium and Veratrum album.

Stomach

Hairball: Usually seen in cats only, it gives rise to digestive disturbances of a very general nature. Inappetance or increase of appetite, occasional vomiting, distended tummy and behavioural changes. It can be removed surgically but infinitely preferable is to help the cat either vomit it or pass it in the faeces if possible. Treatment according to symptoms can be very helpful, for example Colocynth, Colchicum, Gratiola, Nux vomica and Raphanus.

Ornithogallum Ø as a single dose can also be very helpful.

Foreign Bodies of any description in the stomach can be treated similarly.

Neoplastic disease of the stomach may be helped by using one of:

Arsen alb., Hydrastis, Ornithogallum Ø or Phosphorus.

Torsion of the Stomach. Surgery can be averted in some cases if one treats with Ornithogallum Ø and Colocynth or Colchicum along with Aconite. This condition is very serious and sudden and a veterinary surgeon should be consulted immediately.

Hiccough: Especially in young puppies.

With eructation	– Nux vomica.
With yawning or nervous symptoms	– Ignatia.
With yawning	– Cocculus.

Pyloric Disorder: Passage of food on from the stomach is regulated by the Pyloric Sphincter. Stenosis of this organ, from injury, surgery or nervous causes, creates a functional obstruction either partial or complete. Staphisagria is a remedy with particular effect on this structure, especially post-operatively. Consider also Lycopodium, Nux vomica, Ornithogallum Ø and Phosphorus.

Intestines

Worms: Round worms – Abrotanum, Cina, Chenopodium, Santoninum.
Tape Worms – Filix mas., Granatum

It is not yet scientifically proven that these remedies will cause the host to eliminate the parasite. If elimination of worms is required from a public health point of view, etc. unless proof can be found it would be unwise to rely totally on these remedies to do the job. Undoubtedly, however, the disease picture of parasitism can be greatly helped (possibly by restoring the host/parasite balance). Herbal preparations of these remedies are likely to be more effective in causing elimination and Garlic also has a reputation in this field. Work is urgently needed on this topic. Remember also Lecithin or Phos. Acid to aid build-up if debilitated.

Intussusception: Usually needs surgery particularly if advanced but 'symptomatic' homoeopathic treatment could help resolve the condition prior to surgery. Consider:

Chamomilla, Cina, Colchicum, Merc. cor., Nux vom. and Veratrum album.

Colic: This is abdominal pain. The accompanying symptoms help to guide one to the correct remedy.

Associated with teething in young animals	– Chamomilla.
With much tympany	– Colchicum.
	Raphanus.
After overeating	– Nux vomica.
Severe pain, back arched and abdomen cramped	– Colocynth.
Much reaction to noise and touch, grinding of teeth	– Belladonna
	– Mag Phos.
	– Zinc met.
Flatus being passed	– Carbo veg.
Grinding of teeth	– Cina, Plumb met., Podoph.

Foreign Body: Treat as for intussusception. This may aid the passage of the offending object and therefore may avert surgery. Do not delay consulting a veterinary surgeon if symptoms are not removed.

Flatulence: From either end of the digestive tract, consider:

If rich food is cause of trouble   – Nux vomica.
Due to vegetable material in diet   – Carbo veg.

Also consider Calc. carb., Lycopodium.

Hernia: Herniation is the protrusion of abdominal contents
(e.g.) bowel through a natural or accidental aperture in the
body wall. The contents then lie beneath the skin. These
hernias occur most commonly at the umbilicus, the inguinal region and the perineum. They are often caused by raised
abdominal pressure and by an inherent weakness of the
body wall.

Nux vomica or Lycopodium are indicated to try to help
the underlying digestive causes and effects, they can even in
some cases aid reduction of the hernia. In cases of perineal
hernia due to overstraining at the stool consider Alumina or
Nux vomica.

Prostate treatment should be considered here too in male
dogs. A remedy closely associated with inguinal herniation
is Sulphuric acid. Should the hernia become incarcerated or
strangulated this is a very dangerous condition, consider as
first aid Belladonna and Opium.

Veterinary advice should be sought with all forms of
herniation.

Vomiting

This heading is not included under stomach conditions
since the author believes that vomiting is such a potentially
serious condition that it should be under a heading of its
own. It is potentially serious for two reasons:

a) Loss of fluids and electrolytes leading to dehydration – a
   very dangerous condition possibly needing fluid
   therapy.
b) It may be a sign of some other severe illness such as
   Diabetes, Kidney trouble, Jaundice, Parvovirus and
   many others. It may also be the result of obstruction of
   the bowel.

Having said all this by way of caution, there can be many
commonplace causes behind vomiting which, as long as the
vomiting is not prolonged, need not be too serious.

Carnivores will vomit naturally for their offspring. This, of course, requires no treatment.

By far the most common type of vomiting encountered is that of gastritis or gastroenteritis. Treat, as usual, in the homoeopathic manner, that is with regard to concomitant symptoms and the character of the vomit:

Mouth dry, often evidence of allergic– Apis mel.
reaction, seeks fresh air, absence of
thirst.

Simultaneous vomit and diarrhoea– Arsen. alb.
(usually) dry mouth, very restless,
may be blood in vomit or stool,
clear white mucoid vomit (usually)

Intolerence of milk in young animal.– Aethusia.
Milk often vomited as curds and
animal can often be shocked

Repeated reflex vomiting, such as seen– Apomorphine.
in Parvovirus (see p. 117)

Greenish bile vomited after large– Eupatorium
intake of water at one go. Thirst is for perfoliatum
larger quantities at a time

Large thirst, repeated cycles of drink,– Merc. sol.
vomit. Vomit usually yellow, mouth
very wet with saliva

Large thirst, repeated cycle as above– Merc. cor.
but usually more violent, vomit is
usually watery/mucoid

Vomiting very soon after food   – Phosphorus.

Vomiting several hours after rich food– Nux vom.
(usually), stool may be absent or hard

Vomiting several hours after fatty– Pulsatilla.
food (usually)

Simple regurgitation of food   – Ipecacuanha.

Frequent slimy vomiting with much– Ipecacuanha.
retching and pain between bouts

Immediate rejection of food with– Veratrum alb.
frothy yellow vomit at other times

Post operative vomiting   – Nux vomica.

Where 'coffee ground' type vomitus is produced there is evidence of gastric bleeding and this is often of a serious nature for example stomach neoplasia, ulcerated stomach.

Think of Ornithogallum Ø for first aid. Consult a veterinary surgeon immediately.

Travel Sickness: May or may not be accompanied by vomiting but usually there is much drooling of saliva, a fearful or depressed expression of the face and an unwilling- · ness to move.

Petroleum has proved to be very widely curative in this unfortunate and inconvenient condition. Think also of Borax, Cocculus and Tabacum. The misery of travel sickness to the dog and cat is difficult to imagine but should not be allowed to continue, as is often the case, simply because it is non serious and easily explicable.

Diarrhoea

Is more common than vomiting and less often a symptom of serious illness but nonetheless the same words of caution should be applied when undertaking the treatment of diarrhoea (see p. 70). Again treat according to characteristics of the stool and concomitant symptoms.

In choosing a remedy one must consider several important questions. Is there straining before, during or after stool (tenesmus)? Is there flatus with stool? Is there abdominal pain? Is there pain on passing stool? Is the anus sore? Is the stool involuntary or without apparent sensation? One can detect this last symptom by the fact that the animal will pass stools without obvious discomfort and often in small quantities anywhere, anytime. A dog or cat is usually very particular about being clean in the house and, if 'caught short' by a sudden need to produce faeces, will usually produce near a door or on a particular floor surface or mat but involuntary stools are passed indiscriminately.

Pasty diarrhoea, usually painless and– Merc. sol.
non urgent
If there is tenesmus, with a forceful– Merc. cor.
spurt of diarrhoea
Flatus   and   stool   passed– Aloe.
indiscriminately (spluttery) often so
violently that the animal cannot
control where it happens, often mucus
with faeces. May also be involuntary

Tenesmus, bloody or mucoid stools,– often stools watery or frothy, often yellow, also tenesmus with no stool, often brought on by cold and wet conditions	Rhus tox.
Tenesmus, large quantities of stool and flatus produced at a time, stool may be yellowy and liquid or soft and loose	Nat sulph.
Diarrhoea with severe colic with arched back	Colocynth.
Ineffectual urging and jelly like stools	Colchicum.
Flatulent colic (frequently used in acute liver or pancreas conditions)	Iris vers.
Watery, greenish diarrhoea, especially in teething patient	Chamomilla.
Watery, greenish diarrhoea	Eupat. perf.
When diarrhoea has semi-formed solid material in loose stool	Calc. carb. Lycopodium. Ant. crud. Senecio.
When stool is loose, yellow and painless (usually), containing semi-formed solid material	Phos. acid.
When stool is black consider	Crot. hor. Leptandra.
When there is much gurgling and stool is watery and forceful	Croton tig. Podophyllum.
No two stools alike, patient shy, reserved and fussy feeder	Pulsatilla.
Difficulty to produce a small quantity of foul smelling faeces, which is either hard or partly formed with fluid, defaecation is painless (usually) but followed by great weakness	Phosphorus.
Where great debility accompanies diarrhoea, usually with cold state with near collapse use	Camphor. Veratrum alb.
When great debility accompanies diarrhoea also think of	Bryonia. Cuprum met. Rhus tox.

Urgent stool giving rise to panic to– Aloe.
produce stool   Causticum.
                                     Croton tig.
                                     Lilium tig.
                                     Veratrum alb.
To help rebuild the constitution after– China.
debilitating diarrhoea   Phos. acid.

Diarrhoea caused by various aetiological factors can be treated giving significance to those factors:

Severe fright	– Aconite.
General nervousness	– Argent nit.
	Gelsemium.
Injury	– Arnica.
Excessive intake of fruit	– Bryonia.
Excessive intake of rich food	– Nux vomica.
Teething	– Chamomilla.
Cold/wet	– Dulcamara.
	Rhus tox.

Constipation: The failure of defaecation or difficulty in defaecation can be a useful guiding symptom in the choosing of a remedy or it can be a serious symptom in itself. Only while writing this section, I had cause to treat a Bassett Hound with quite severe post operative depression, painful urination, failure to pass faeces, vomiting with great distress (caused by overworking the abdominal wound during retching) and general malaise. Nux vomica was chosen using the post operative constipation as a guiding symptom and within four hours the bitch had freely passed faeces (of a very hard nature) and had ceased vomiting. Nux vomica is also of help where there is much urging with the constipation such as in cases of prostatis with perineal herniation.

When stool cannot be passed with straining, whether the stool be soft or hard and dry	– Alumina.
When stool is large and painful and anus is red (often skin involvement and a dislike of heat)	– Sulphur.
'Shy' stool, that is stool which comes half way out and recedes	– Silicea. Thuja.

Very chalky stool, sometimes result of eating bones	– Calc. carb.
If liver dysfunction has given rise to constipation	– Sepia.
Post operative constipation	– Nux vomica.
Key Gaskell Syndrome	– See p. 120

Anal Prolapse: Can occur with diarrhoea or constipation and depending on concomitant symptoms, one should consider:
Aloe, Apis mel., Ignatia, Merc corr., Nux vomica, Podophyllum, Ruta grav. and Sepia.
If bleeding from the anus, Aesculus and Nitric acid are usually very effective.

Anal Furunculosis may be helped by Calc sulph or Silicea.

Anal gland problems will be dealt with under skin troubles.

Liver and Pancreas

Problems of the liver and pancreas are usually of a severe enough nature to warrant full veterinary attention. Homoeopathic remedies can be extremely valuable.

For complaints of the **gall bladder** particularly think of Berberis.

General **liver** remedies are Berberis, Chelidonium and Lycopodium. (See also Hepatitis qv).

Pain in the **liver region** think of such remedies as Aesculus, Chionanthus, Phosphorus and Sepia.

Where there is **jaundice** think of:

Aesculus, Carduus mar., Chelidonium, Hydrastis, Merc sol. and Phosphorus.

Where the liver is overloaded by over-eating of **rich food** Nux vomica is a great help.

The **pancreas** when diseased gives rise to two sets of problems, the first is digestive and the second metabolic.
a) **Pancreatic Insufficiency:** Gives rise to failure to digest fats and proteins in the bowel leading to diarrhoea which is usually yellow. Homoeopathic remedies can help here, consider Chionanthus or Senecio. Diarrhoea and weight loss are associated with this condition and Iodum and Phosphoric acid fit these symptoms very well. It

may still be necessary to supplement the diet with pancreatic enzymes for a while. Tripe is also a good food, providing a supply of digestive enzymes as well as being a natural food for dogs.

b) **Diabetes Mellitus:** The failure of the insulin producing capacity of the pancreas gives rise to this condition which is a disturbance of the glucose metabolism in the tissue cells and the blood. Sugar also appears in the urine. Insulin in low potency and Iris versicolor, Phos. acid, Syzigium and Uranium nit. can all help to reduce symptoms and reduce urine sugar output.

The pancreas can also suffer from acute inflammation (or **Pancreatitis**) and this is treated symptomatically. Aconite, Atropinum, Iris versicolor and Phosphorus can all help in this condition which is very serious and troublesome.

The Urinary System

Conditions affecting any part of the urinary system, whose major function is the elimination of toxic materials and by-products from the blood, are potentially very dangerous and therefore veterinary advice should be sought in any such case. In this section only the homoeopathic treatment of such conditions shall be discussed, not the very important nursing side.

The most common conditions are inflammation of the kidney (Nephritis) and irritation of the bladder (Cystitis). The latter manifests itself as a frequent desire to urinate producing small quantities often, much tenesmus, pain and sometimes blood in the urine. This should not be confused with a blocked urinary system although the symptoms are similar. In the first there is usually an empty badder and in the second a full bladder. Failure to correctly distinguish between the similar symptoms will lead to a tragic outcome so all pet owners should seek veterinary advice. Prostate problems in dogs may also present as urinary problems but must be distinguished (see Male Sexual System).

Cystitis
Burning pain, frequent attempts at– Cantharis.
micturition and bloody urine
Similar to above but less often indicated– Merc corr.

Where overdistension is the cause of– Causticum.
cystitis
With neuromuscular involvement– Nux vomica.
(e.g. post operative)
Copious sediment in the urine – Chimaphila.
Tenesmus and (sometimes) urinary– Equisetum.
incontinence, with much straining
after urinating, can be haematuria

Blood in the urine although usually symptomatic of urinary problems may not always be so. Defects of the clotting mechanism or injury to the kidneys may also give rise to blood in urine. The latter one should treat with Arnica. the former (e.g. Warfarin poisoning) see Circulatory System.

As either the cause or effect of cystitis, **urinary calculi** can give rise to problems. They can create a blockage of the urinary system at any point but mostly this occurs in the male dog at the level of the os penis. It also occurs in bitches and dogs as a result of large stones blocking the neck of the bladder and in cats, especially male, in the urethra. Calc. carb., Calc. phos. or Lycopodium should be a routine treatment of canine cases while investigations are carried out according to constitution. Berberis, Benz. acid and Pareira are all effective remedies also.

Sabulous plugs in the male cat respond well to Sarsaparilla and Thlaspi bursa.

When blockage has occurred as a result of injury and ensuing oedema, use Arnica and Apis mel.

Nephritis: This is a very difficult condition to treat in the advanced stages, but in the earlier stages responds well to such remedies as Ammonium carb., Arsen alb., Baptisia, Berberis, Kali. chlor., Mercurius, Nat. mur., Plumbum met., Phosphorus and Urtica urens.

Since kidney problems are so serious it is very necessary to know the various symptoms associated with these remedies to get a good result. This book has not the scope to cover these fully so you are referred to any good materia medica to obtain closer details. Some details are given in Chapter 17 to help match concomitant symptoms to remedies. Veterinary attention should be sought.

Urinary Incontinence: This can occur as a result of cystitis (see p. 76), age or the ovarohysterectomy operation. With the latter I have had mixed success (possibly due to the animal no longer being 'normal') but try:

Calc. fluor., Causticum, Nux vomica, Silicea, Staphysagria and Thiosinaminum from the physical point of view. (See p. 86).
Stilboestrol in low potency, Sepia or Ustilago maydis from the hormonal point of view.

For age incontinence try:

Agnus castus, Causticum, Thiosinaminum or Turnera.

Male Sexual System

The most frequent problem met in the surgery related to the male sexual system is a behavioural one: that of **Hypersexuality**. The young dog especially about 1½ to 2 years old becomes vagrant, peevish, overboisterous, slightly unreliable and urinates territorially, including inside the house. This problem can also lead to prostate problems, cystitis, paraphismosis, injury from jumping fences and car accidents. It is generally antisocial and can suffer injury by the hand of offended owners of other dogs or property.

In many cases Gelsemium can help as also can Phosphorus, Tarentula hisp. and Zincum met.

Weakness can occur as a result of this problem, consider Conium or Picric acid.

Although primarily female remedies, Pulsatilla and Sepia may help some dogs, according to constitution.

Where **convulsions** or extreme excitement with **salivation** occurs consider:

Chamomilla, Gelsemium, Ignatia, Lyssin, Nux vomica or Zincum.

Paraphimosis (prolonged erection with or without strangulation of the penis) can occur and here Jacaranda, Picric acid or Selenium can be of great help.

Prostatic problems are common and can occur in the older male dog for no apparent reason or the younger dog for the above reasons.

Older dogs are often helped by	– Agnus Castus Conium Ferr pic., Pulsatilla., Sabal serr., Selenium.
Where difficulty is encountered passing faeces	– Nux vomica, Thuja.
Where difficulty is encountered passing urine	– Merc. corr., Cantharis.
With emissions of blood	– Ipecac, Nit. Ac.,
Especially helpful to younger dogs	– Sabal serr., Staphysagria.
Also helpful for younger dogs especially with intermittent thin jets of urine often with skin complaints	– Clematis erecta.
Also helpful for younger dogs especially if underweight and passes urine in a slow stream	– Baryta carb.

Inflammation of the Penis and Prepuce occurs not infrequently and one should treat according to symptoms considering such remedies as:

Belladonna, Hepar sulph. and Merc sol.

(Calendula lotion infusions are often a great help and should not be forgotten for topical application on any sore inflamed area).

Inflammation or Swelling of the Testicles is not often seen but depending on the cause and appearance one can treat with:

In case of injury	– Arnica, Bellis perennis.
When acute inflammation is present	– Aconite, Belladonna, Pulsatilla, Rhododendron.
When the testes are indurated and smaller than normal (usually in the aged dog)	– Agnus castus, Clematis, Conium, Iodum.

79

Retained Testicle or Monorchidism or Cryptorchidism is seen fairly frequently.

One should think in terms of:

Baryta carb., Calc carb., Clematis, Testosterone in low frequency and Thyroidinum.

Deficient Sexual Power is mostly noticed in the stud dog and is rare.

Testosterone in low potency can help as can Agnus castus, Conium, Lycopodium, Phos. acid, Sabal serr. and Selenium.

Where the penis is extruded but desire is absent try Yohimbinum.

The Castrated Male Dog and Cat have their own particular problems.

DOG   Bilateral hair loss on the sides of the body and problems with overweight predominate. One should always consider Testosterone in low potency and Agnus castus. Food intake should be restricted if obesity is occurring (see Obesity p. 113 and Female p. 86).

Where problems of **hair loss** are encountered one should consider apart from Testosterone:

Thallium acetas, Thyroid in low potency and Ustilago maydis.

CAT   Skin problems are of especial importance here, the most common being 'Miliary Eczema'. Progesterone or Testosterone in low potency should be considered as too should Pulex, the potentised flea, which can help enormously in some cases. The lesions' character should also help to guide one to homoeopathic remedies here. For example:

Antimonium crud, Antimonium tart., Arsen alb, Cicuta, Dulcamara, Graphites, Lycopodium, Mezereum, Muriatic acid, Natrum mur., Phosphorus, Rhus tox., Sulphur, Thallium and Zinc met have all been used with varying success. Think constitutionally. (see also p. 138 and p. 140).

As a general note all problems associated with neutering in the cat or dog, male or female, seem to be difficult to treat homoeopathically and some appear to be completely refractory. One could hypothesise that the patient is no longer normal and homoeopathy works best through the normal system.

Female Sexual System

Under this umbrella are gathered conditions affecting the ovaries, womb and mammary glands, fertility problems, problems of pregnancy, parturition and motherhood and finally lactation. The part the female plays in the continuation of life in mammals is far greater than that played by the male so this heading will embrace many more topics and much more information than was contained in the section on the male. More problems are encountered in bitches than queens.

Ovaries, Cyclicity, Infertility, Behavioural Problems associated with Ovarian Cycle:

Remedies having a particular effect on the functioning of the ovaries, on the behaviour associated with this and on fertility are:

Sepia — A remedy for the bitch who is moody, morose, over protective, sometimes vicious. This description fits the symptoms of false pregnancy in many bitches and should always be considered in this condition.

Pulsatilla — Is a remedy to be used in similar connections to Sepia but much more open, sunny natured, yielding type of bitches who are up and down in their moods, show a variable appetite, and have a shy nature. Variability is the byword of Pulsatilla (the wind flower) and variable it is in this context. A creamy vulval discharge is often present after Oestrus.

Platina — For the haughty detached mentality, who can be highly strung.

Lachesis — Is very much like Sepia. It has a predilection for the throat area, and for the left side of the patient. Jealousy is predominant in the symptoms, and suspicion. There is often much bleeding of dark blood at oestrus and the mammary glands can show a purplish tinge.

Iodum — Can be of use particularly in thinner subjects to encourage a bitch to display oestrus, if retarded.

Palladium — Is effective in those who brighten-up enormously when with the owner for going out but sink into apathy when left alone. It is a right sided remedy.

Lilium tig — Suits the overanxious, depressed bitch who is always on the move. Often there is a rheumatic appearance to the walk.
This animal does not enjoy a fuss and likes to be left alone.

Murex — Applies mostly to queens and rarely to bitches when a condition of nymphomania is present, that is, she is repeatedly calling. She is always lively, nervous and affectionate. Ferula gluaca, Gratiola and Origanum should also be remembered in this connection.

I shall refer to many of these predominantly female constitutional remedies again and again in this section so refer back to these pages for clarification of the indications for use of the remedies. (Also Chapter 17).

After the heat period in the bitch a **'false pregnancy'** period is usual. This may or may not show itself but can display anything from nearly no signs to a full imitation of the pregnant state from conception to birth, including mammary development with milk. More often than not, when there are signs they are of a moody disposition with variable milk production. Often a 'nest' is made and the bitch guards it. Sepia or Pulsatilla according to the disposition of the bitch could be used. To aid the drying up of secretions of milk, do not massage the glands but give remedies such as Bryonia, Calc carb, Cyclamen, Pulsatilla and Urtica (the latter in low potency).

Also after the heat period, often about six weeks later, a bitch may become polydypsic and off colour. There may or may not be a vaginal discharge. This heralds the condition

pyometra which is potentially exceedingly serious and can require Ovarohysterectomy. In severe stages the bitch can become toxic, dehydrated, suffer kidney damage and even die.

Homoeopathic treatments in the earlier stages can help tremendously but veterinary advice should be sought. Remedies such as Aletris, Caulophyllum, Pulsatilla, Sabina and Sepia and, in cases where there is toxicity and vomiting, Echinacea, have all been used with degrees of success varying from 100 per cent to not enough to avert surgery. Much must depend on the speed of onset, the severity and the duration before treatment. Pulsatilla is not so likely to be used for this condition since Pulsatilla patients rarely display great thirst.

Problems of Pregnancy, Parturition and the Post Partum Period. More of this text applies to the bitch than the queen although remedies are as effective in either. It appears however that the bitch needs more attention than the queen at this time. It is worth remembering that when any creature is pregnant, be that creature human, canine, feline or whatever, any food, drug, vaccine, etc. administered will affect both mother and offspring. It is here that homoeopathy has especial advantage over conventional medicine (see also Preventive Medicine in Chapter 14). One should always avoid vaccinations during this sensitive period and try to avoid the use of any drugs.

Pregnancy in the bitch and queen is usually uneventful but Caulophyllum should always be given towards the end of pregnancy (about three times weekly for the last two weeks) to ease the impending birth process. Where abortion is threatened Viburnum has a great reputation and one can also use the nosodes of any specific infective agents, which may be involved in the cause, to prevent abortion. Cobaltum nitricum also has a reputation where repeated abortion occurs in an individual. Debility after abortion can be helped by Kali carb.

During the birth process Caulophyllum is again indicated and Calc phos to improve the tonicity of the womb. Any difficulties at this stage can be dramatically helped by these remedies. Pulsatilla and Sepia can also be used to help some of the mental side of the problem. Gossypium or Secale can be of value when a bitch giving birth to a lot of puppies becomes exhausted (also think of Cuprum acet. in these circumstances).

Should a Caesarean section be necessary despite these efforts, remember Arnica, Secale and Staphisagria to aid the post-operative recovery (see also Post Operative Remedies p. 113).

When a delivery has been traumatic for the mother always remember Bellis per., or Apis mell where urination is difficult as a result of oedema. Remember the offspring too, Arnica is of great value here and consider Baryta carb., Helleborus, Hypericum, Laurocerasus and Nat. sulph. where necessary (see materia medica, Chapter 17 and Injury p. 111). Sometimes offspring and mother suffer from the anaesthetic administered and one should bear in mind the relevant potentised anaesthetic and Opium. When a puppy or kitten is cold and collapsed use Carbo veg. (see also Puppy Problems p. 131).

Post Partum involution of the womb and expulsion of membranes and debris is encouraged by Caulophyllum.

Haemorrhage post partum is rarely a problem in the dog and cat but can be helped by the following remedies according to the character of the bleeding (see Haemorrhage p. 109 and materia medica):

Aconite	Hamamellis	Sabina
Aletris	Ipecacuanha	Secale
Crocus	Lachesis	Thlaspi bursa
Crotalus	Nitric acid	Ustilago
Ferrum met		

Retained Afterbirth is also rare but consider:

Caulophyllum, Lilium tig., Pulsatilla, Sabina, Sepia and Ustilago. Think constitutionally.

If toxaemia arises consider Echinacea or Pyrogen.

Mismothering or a failure of the maternal behaviour to correctly 'switch on' consider:

Lachesis, Lilium tig., Platina, Pulsatilla and Sepia.

They have all been used successfully using the homoeopathic method for selection of a remedy (see p. 81).

Failure to produce enough milk for the puppies or kittens is a relatively more common condition. Consider here such remedies as:

Calc. carb., Calc. phos., Lecithin, Medusa and Urtica (the latter in high potency).

Conium, Iodum and Sabal serr. will encourage an underdeveloped mammary gland.

A few days after giving birth several conditions may arise.

Eclampsia, a disturbance of the Calcium metabolism occurs in some cases and is characterised by a range of symptoms from restlessness through to collapse in tetany. There is usually very rapid breathing. Calc. phos. and Mag. phos. are primary remedies here. Arsen alb., Belladonna, Cicuta, Hyoscyamus, Ignatia, Lilium tig., Stramonium and Zinc can all be used according to symptoms and Hydrocyanic acid where there is much cyanosis. Intravenous injection of Calcium is a must if symptoms are prolonged since the mother can die from this condition, so veterinary attention is essential. Calc. phos. prior to confinement can help avoid this condition.

Mastitis can develop soon after parturition or after weaning. Here think of:

Apis mell., Belladonna, Bryonia, Phytolacca and Urtica, according to symptoms shown. There are several proprietary compounds on sale in France where various of these are mixed together. This precaution is to avoid the risk of failure due to incorrect prescribing and a high success rate is claimed. Veterinary attention should be sought.

Metritis is an inflammation, and probably an infection, of the womb following parturition and usually shows a vulval discharge. According to the condition of the mother and the character of the discharge one should consider:

Caulophyllum, Pulsatilla, Sabina, Secale, Sepia and Ustilago.

Remember also:

Baptisia, Echinacea or Pyrogen if septicaemia or toxaemia results.

Nipples can exhibit some problems, for example cracked and sore nipples from sucking puppies or kittens consider Graphites by mouth and Calendula lotion on the nipples.

Inverted Nipples can be helped by Sarsaparilla or Silicea and these remedies should be given in limited doses before the end of pregnancy or, better, before mating if the condition is noticed at the time.

Weaning puppies or kittens can result in the mother having too much milk and the mammae becoming engorged. The flow of milk can be reduced with low potency Urtica or Cyclamen but be warned of mastitis developing as a result of this engorgement of the glands, consider also Conium. Ignatia will help the mental problems associated with weaning (for problems in offspring at this time see p. 131) and Calc. carb., China, Kali carb. or Lecithin will help to build up body condition again.

Mammary Tumours may develop in older bitches and queens whether or not they have had puppies or kittens. Homoeopathy makes no extravagant claims that it can cure these completely, but they can in some cases be controlled and, in a few cases cured. The following remedies all have a reputation in this field:

Arsen alb., Asterias, Calc. fluor., Calc. iod., Chimaphila, Conium, Hydrastis, Phosphorus, Phytolacca and Thuja.

One should think of Phosphorus where there is suppuration and Asterias if there is ulceration. Remember constitution and diet.

Problems of the Ovarohysterectomy Female. They are MILIARY ECZEMA in cats (see p. 80 but think of low potency Oestrogen and Progesterone) and in bitches OVERWEIGHT and URINARY INCONTINENCE. OBESITY leads one to think of Calc. carb. or Pulsatilla as a remedy but where there is a tendency to skin trouble as well think of Graphites or Sulphur. Ant. crud. or Anacardium can help real gluttons. Alopecia may also be a problem.

URINARY INCONTINENCE as a result of 'spaying' can be a very refractory condition to treat. Consider Oestrogen in low potency or Causticum, Gelsemium, Sabal serr., Turnera and Ustilago (see also p. 78).

Respiratory System

Upper Respiratory Problems commonly encountered are coughs, cat flu (see nose), sinusitis (see nose), sore throats (see mouth) and laryngitis (which usually takes the form of a changed voice).

Lower Respiratory Problems include difficulty in breathing and coughs.

Cough. This is usually the response to irritation in the larynx, trachea or lungs as a result of foreign body aspiration or inflammation from, for example, infection. Beware however of the 'heart' type of cough (see heart) or worms. Upper respiratory coughs are generally less serious than lower respiratory coughs and generally a harsher sound but always, in homoeopathy, one treats according to the symptoms not the diagnosis of specific diseases. Beware of the potentially serious nature of some coughs. Veterinary advice should be sought if at all in doubt.

Dogs and cats rarely display the character of sputum so all there is to go on usually is the type of cough and the modalities. Major remedies are:

Dry spasmodic cough	– Belladonna, Bryonia, Cuprum, Drosera, Pertussin, Stannum, Sticta.
Cough with vomit	– Ipecacuanha.
Cough with retching	– Drosera, Nux vomica.
Hoarseness	– Bryonia (worse for movement), Causticum, Phosphorus.
Dry teasing cough	– Aconite, Nux vomica, Pulsatilla, Rhus tox.
Rattling cough	– Ant tart, Dulcamara, Ferrum phos., Stannum.
Choked cough	– Spongia.
With dyspnoea	– Ammon. carb., Ant. tart., Arsen. alb., Kali carb., Lycopodium, Phosphorus, Spongia.
With fluid mucus	– Coccus.

If **Kennel Cough** is suspected then in addition to similium remember the nosode (see Chapter 11.)

Asthmatic breathing   – Apis mell. (a strong desire for fresh air, usually lung congestion)
Arsen. alb. (restless).
Aspidosperma Ø,
Lobelia inflata,
Spongia (worse for heat),
Sulphur (worse for heat and usually skin problems too).

Asphyxia   – Ant. tart. (phlegmy and blue), Apis mell. (if oedema of throat is cause), Carbo veg. (blueness and very cold), Laurocerasus Ø (blueness)

All these symptoms of cough and troubled breathing may be result of heart problems and are, therefore, potentially very serious. Consult your veterinary surgeon.

Cat Flu see Chapter 8 – Nose and Chapter 11 – Specifics.

The Heart, Circulatory System and Blood

In all cases of heart trouble veterinary advice should be sought as the professional can assess cardiac problems and their response to treatment. The following remedies have been found to be of use.

In case of heart weakness   – Crataegus Ø, Digitalis in low potency, Strophanthus Ø.

In cases of heart cough   – Naja. Prunus v. Spongia.

In cases of Angina   – Aconite with: Cactus or Cimicifuga.

Thudding heart   – Lycopus.
In cases of Arrhythmia   – Convallaria Ø.
If heart is slow and pulse weak,   – Viscum album.
Valvular conditions, heart often oversized
Very good in valvular disorders   – Adonis vernalis.
In cases of cyanosis   – Laurocerasus Ø.

In cases of **acute failure** there is much distress. Here Aconite, Ant.tart., Arsen. Alb. and Carbo veg. can help the situation according to the symptoms.

Ascites or Dropsy is the name given to the accumulation of fluid in the abdomen. This can arise from several causes (see Feline Infectious Peritonitis p. 120 and Lymphatic System p. 89) but is commonly caused by right ventricular heart failure, or swollen liver.

Adonis vernalis, Apis mell., Apocynum and Digitalis have all been used with degrees of success. All these remedies have a strongly diuretic action and, with the exception of Apis, help the heart directly too.

Pulmonary Congestion from a similar problem on the left side of the heart is greatly helped by Apis mel., Arsen alb. and Spongia (see also Asthmatic Breathing p. 88).

Anaemia and Haemorrhage see Generalities p. 107 and 109.

The Lymphatic System (Reticulo-Endothelial System)

This consists of the lymph ducts alongside all the veins, the lymph nodes at various sites in the body and the major lymphatic duct back to the heart. Their function is to drain from the tissues fluid which has left the blood vessels. They also form an important part of the defence mechanisms of the body, supplying antibody defences and defensive filtration in the lymph nodes. The spleen, bone marrow and liver are also involved and the Thymus in the very young. The tonsils are also part of this system (see sore throats pp. 65 & 66).

Generalised swelling of all the lymph glands can be helped by:

Arsen alb., Arsen iod., Arum triph., Baryta Iod., Calc fluor., Cistus can., Iodum and Lapis albus according to symptoms.

If it is a form of lymphosarcoma that is manifesting itself in this way then the prognosis may be grave.

Lymph nodes swollen in the throat region often accompanied by a sore throat (see p. 66) are helped by Mercurial remedies, Baryta carb and Calc fluor. For indurated glands think of Cistus, Conium or Lapis.

When lymph nodes in particular parts of the body (e.g. inguinal region) are enlarged it is usually a sign of neoplasia or infection in the parts distal to that gland.

For infected parts use Hepar sulph. Neoplasia presents greater problems, see p. 112.

Locomotor System

(Which is taken to mean all parts of the musculo skeletal system apart from the head which has already been mentioned p. 50).

Skeletal Problems – Bones and Joints

Young dogs (and, more rarely, cats) can suffer from incorrect bone metabolism leading to large epiphyseal swellings ('knobbly' legs and ribs), bone deformities as a result of softening and often lameness. The joints fail to form correctly and permanent disability throughout life can result. Calcium and other mineral supplementation and vitamins A, C and D are known to help control the problem but homoeopathically one can help tremendously with Calc. phos. or Calc. fluor. (see also p. 131).

Calc. carb. is more useful if the puppy is very fat in appearance.

Silicea also helps to form connective tissues properly and can be a long term help. In the very debilitated puppy or kitten use Phos. acid as well.

Phos. acid should always be remembered in debility especially rapidly growing undernourished young patients.

Where sore joints are suspected remember Ruta grav. and excessive exercise should be avoided.

In older pups nearing adulthood where one can see that they are late developers use:

In lean dogs	– Calc. phos.
In those still with puppy fat and physically soft, to help complete their maturity	– Calc. carb.

Where they have clearly outgrown	– Calc. fluor.
themselves and are threatened by over	Phos. acid.
exertion (there is a great temptation to	
over exercise the young undermature dog)	

Dwarfism, a separate problem, can be helped by Iodum, Thuja or A.C.T.H. in potency.

Bony Lumps (exostoses) are not uncommon and the treatment of choice here is usually Hekla lava, but consider also Calc. fluor. and Silicea (see also Head p. 50).

Another 'nutritional' osteopathy is that occuring in kidney disease, often called **osteodystrophy,** which manifests itself as a softening of the bone. It results from impaired mineral metabolism as a result of malfunctioning kidneys. Treat the patient constitutionally.

An excellent remedy for hardening the bone and helping mineralisation is Calc. fluor., Hekla lava also helps in this respect.

Osteoporosis is a demincralisation of bone occurring with age. Similar treatment is advisable remembering also Calc. carb., Calc. phos. and Silicea.

Osteomyelitis is an inflammation, usually from infection, of the medulla of the bone. Veterinary attention should be sought.
Hepar. sulph. is of paramount importance here in controlling infection and then consider helping the bone tissues with Ruta grav. (periosteum), Calc. fluor. (bone itself) and Symphytum. The relevant nosode is also very helpful.

Fractures of Bone (see also Injury p. 111) are always helped by Symphytum and Ruta grav. Use of these remedies will usually prevent the 'non-union' phenomenon. Calc phos and Silicea also help the bone metabolism. One should always remember the mental and soft tissue effects of broken bones and give Aconite if there is a lot of fear and always Arnica.

Injury to Bone which doesn't cause a fracture can lead to exostoses (see p. 90) but Arnica and Ruta will help to prevent any such occurrence Symphytum is also of value (see also Injury p. 111). If exostoses occur, use Hekla.

Injury to Joints (see also Injury p. 111) always remember Arnica with Rhus tox. and Ruta grav.

Luxation (dislocation) of joints is a serious injury but after reduction treat as above.

Subluxation is the name given to poorly formed joints which do not articulate correctly. A classical example here is **Hip Dysplasia**. In this condition the ball and socket joint of the hip varies from slightly abnormal on X ray to extremely shallow and almost non-existent. The result is hind leg weakness and Arthritis. Colocynth and the appropriate arthritic treatment (see below) help enormously. Remember too Calc. carb. or Calc. phos. in young dogs. Some small breeds have a similar problem with the **Patella** (knee cap) and I have found Gelsemium to help in this connection again with the appropriate arthritis remedy. (Subluxation may also occur as a result of injury.)

Spinal Problems (see also Hind Leg weakness (p. 93) and Paralysis p. 96)

Disc lesions, Lumbar spasm and any other pain in this region	– Berberis v.
Where urination is difficult	– Causticum.
Where defaecation is difficult	– Nux. vomica.

Also Hypericum, Plumbum, Phosphorus and Ruta grav. have been found to be helpful. This condition occurs especially in Dachshunds.

Where arthritis of the vetebrae or exostoses are considered to be instrumental in the cause of the condition think also of Causticum, Hekla lava, Rhus tox. and Ruta grav. Angustura vera is also a useful adjunct to treatment to prevent nerve damage. Such patients should be resolutely rested and, after the acute state, help may be sought from an Osteopath or Chiropractor. Acupuncture also has a great reputation in this field, and can prove invaluable.

Inflammation of the Joints known by the emotive name of **Arthritis,** produces varying symptoms both locally in the joints and generally (manifested as lameness). Much is lost to the veterinary homoeopath in this sphere in that 'character of pain' is an important prescribing point but that cannot be divined. Local signs at the joint include swelling, pain on palpitation, deformation, pain on movement of joint, fluid, skin changes, etc. The lameness varies in its symptoms and this is important, many questions need to be asked, for example:

Is the lameness worse for movement or better for movement, worse with heat or cold or better for heat or cold, is it worse at the end of a rest after long period of exercise? Does the lameness seem to bother the animal badly or is it just a nuisance? Is it the result of a specific injury? Has the patient a temperature indicating infected arthritis (here the relevant nosode would be a useful adjunct to any symptomatic treatment eg Streptococci, Staphylococci)? Is it an acute arthritis or a chronic longstanding case? (See also Post Op p. 113).

Acute and chronic Arthritis are not treated as separate entities but one would use different dosage regimes. One would not expect a very rapid cure in a chronic case and would use less frequent dosing, but one would require rapid response in an acute case (thereby preventing the tendency to become chronic) so would give frequent doses in a day. Both cases would be treated according to symptoms. In infected cases remember the nosodes with Hepar sulph along with Aconite or Belladonna in acute cases and Silicea in chronic cases. Ledum is indicated if an injury with a sharp penetrating object has occurred, and Arnica in any case of injury. Rhus tox. and Ruta grav. are also very good remedies in injury to joints, aiding healing of the fibrous tissues and prevention of sequelae. Diet is of especial importance.

'Symptomatic' Treatment of Arthritic Problems: (see also Muscular Problems p. 95 and Chapter 17).

Joint pain and lameness worse just– Rhus tox. after rest and especially after resting and after exercise. The patient 'limbers up' and lameness can disappear entirely on exercise. This does not mean a patient must be exercised since, in the long run, failure to rest will lessen the chances of healing. Rhus patients are also worse in cold damp weather.

This is the second remedy of great– Bryonia.
repute in this condition. Its symptoms
are worse for movement and warmth.
At first sight it is the exact opposite of
Rhus tox and it is for this reason that
these two remedies above all others are
assumed to cover the whole spectrum
of arthritis symptoms. This is
however, not the case. Where neither
is effective many others can fit the
picture.

Symptoms worse in changeable– Dulcamara.
Autumn weather (and to a lesser
extent, Spring), worse at night, similar
to Rhus in response to movement.
Skin and diarrhoea symptoms may
coexist.

Usually in the small joints and can– Caulophyllum.
often start up in pregnancy. The neck
can also be affected, often turning to
the left.

Those growing pains that can so often– Calc. phos.
trouble the 6 month to 1 year old dog.
Also conditions of the joints which
arise in pregnancy (see also
Caulophyllum).

Severe pain, sometimes joint– Causticum.
deformities, weakness of muscles
tending almost to paralysis.
Unsteadiness of legs. Better with
damp warmth, worse dry cold.

Worse for movement and in warm– Colchicum.
weather (see also Bryonia) and at
night. Oedema of legs.

Where visible changes occur at the joints consider:

Oedematous swelling of joints, skin– Apis.
has a shiny appearance worse for heat,
touch and pressure and desires fresh
air. Better for cold bathing.

Swellings of joints and joint– Colchicum.
deformities

Where exostoses are evident   – Calc. fluor.
                                             – Hekla lava.

No specific mention has been made of such conditions as **Osteochondritis Dissecans** since symptomatic remedies (as above) and rest are usually sufficient treatment.

Muscular Problems

Injury (trauma) to muscles should always receive Arnica or Bellis perennis (especially the pelvic area). One should also remember, in the case of tendons, Rhus tox. and Ruta grav.

Overexertion (and therefore fatigue and bruising) indicates Arnica. Pulled muscles also require Rhus tox.

In the case of the overworked dog remember too Calc phos or Phos acid. The trauma of parturition can be treated with Bellis in preference to Arnica.

'Rheumatic' conditions should be treated in a similar way to Arthritic conditions (ie symptomatically) and many of the remedies are used for either (often a differential diagnosis is academic) see p. 93. However where no apparent joint involvement can be detected serious disability can occur and a few extra remedies can be called into play:

Pains worse for cold, better for– Cimifuga rac.
warmth especially stiffness of neck and (Actaea rac.)
back. There is usually marked
agitation.

With varying degrees of weakness:

A classic old dog remedy, particularly– Conium.
the old Alsatian, indicated by a
progressive weakness of the hind legs
for no apparent reason.
Shows similar signs to Conium, but– Lithium carb.
the joints are often affected.
Showing progressive weakness of the– Causticum.
limbs, joints can be affected.
Similar but often with alopecia   – Thallium.

Tendency to paralysis [see also CDRM (p. 103)]

Where one group of muscles in- particular is involved	Plumbum.
Where a widespread paralysis is- evident, usually of a spastic nature (see also Fits p. 101).	Lathyrus.
Where 'rheumatism' has led to- paralysis /	Causticum. Rhus tox. Phosphorus.
Where spinal problems are suspected –	Conium. Lathyrus.
Where spinal problems are suspected- in Hypersexual states.	Picric acid.

Muscular trembling (cross reference here with Nervous System)

Old dogs	– Calc. phos. Kali phos. Phosphorus.
Excitement	– Mercurius.
Anticipation	– Kali brom.
Exertion	– Rhus tox.
After defaecation, usually in older dogs	– Conium.

Skin

In the realm of skin diseases it is sad to say homoeopathic treatment runs into much difficulty as does conventional therapy. However, the successes are very encouraging despite failures and efforts to take the work of this section further can only improve the situation. Two reasons leap to mind for the failure in the treatment of skins. One is the likelihood that, since animal skin is so different from human, remedies would have different provings in animals with regard to skin. The other is the very important fact that the skin is the largest organ of the body, and although only able to manifest disease in a few ways, more often than not reflects a deep internal problem (mental or physical) the nature of which is not easy to detect, especially in animals. The all too obvious skin problems are seen, but it is very difficult to look beyond to see the whole patient problem from which they arise even if it is suspected that such a problem exists for one tends to think mostly in terms of contact allergy, ectoparasites, bacterial or fungal infections, dermatitis from chemical irritants, hormonal problems, trauma and self inflicted trauma (see Appendix 8). It is when one opens one's mind to the vast dustbin of 'idiopathic' skin diseases (arising from no apparent cause) that one starts to search around for involvement within the animal's metabolism and psyche. The skin is a whole body organ and is very sensitive to whole body conditions. Thus, sometimes, the only symptoms of disease of the whole body are skin symptoms. The answer to more effective homoeopathic skin treatment must lie in striving to remember this.

When psychological (mental) causes for skin complaints (whatever the symptom) are suspected refer to Chapter 12 on Mental Conditions.

When after-effects (sometimes long lived) of specific infectious diseases are suspected use the relevant nosode.

When after-effects of vaccination are suspected, again use the relevant nosode and Pulsatilla, Sulphur or Thuja. (See p. 143). This is a common trigger for skin problems.

When hormonal problems are suspected, use the relevant hormone in potency and Iodum, Ustilago or Thallium and the relevant symptomatic remedy.

Where metabolic problems are suspected (e.g. in liver dysfunction use Berberis, Lycopodium, Phosphorus, Nux vomica or Chelidonium) refer to relevant section of this book.

Where a specific allergy is diagnosed use of the potentised preparation of the allergen (e.g. House Dust, Fleas or Grasses) may be helpful.

Where Neoplasia exists refer to section on Neoplasia p. 112.

Where dietary problems are suspected the diet should be corrected. Homoeopathic potencies of the dietary minerals greatly help the animal to adjust its metabolism of that mineral. (See p. 37).

In all cases a remedy to match the SYMPTOMS (see below) may be used. (However if ectoparasites or ring-worm are involved it may not be sufficient to rely only on a homoeopathic remedy.) *Always remember the constitutional approach, this is a whole body disorder.*

'Symptomatic' Treatment of Skin Disorders

The choice of remedy must, in the final instance, rest with one's knowledge of the materia medica of the remedies. Chapter 17 only provides a very basic materia medica. For a wider knowledge of the remedies consult other works such as Clarke, Boericke, Kent or Tyler. Only by reading different authors can one begin to get a valuable working knowledge of remedies. The following are given as useful suggestions. *Constitutional principles are very important.*

Allergic type swellings (Urtiearin) (p. 107)	–Apis, Astacus, Bovista, Chamomilla, Medusa, Potentised allergens, Pulex, Urtica.
Alopecia	–Alumen, Arsen alb., Kali ars., Lycopodium., Nat. mur., Pix liquida, Selenium, Thallium, Ustilago.
Anal Adenomata	–Thuja.
Anal Glands	–Calendula lotion, Hepar sulph., Sanicula, Silicea, Tarentula. cub.
Bends of limbs	–Aethusia, Ammonium carb, Ant. crud., Graphites, Kali arsen., Lycopodium, Nat. mur., Sepia.
Blackened skin	–Berberis, Kali arsen., Lachesis, Sepia, Sulphanilamide.
Bruises	–See Injury p. 112.
Burns	–See p. 108.
Cracks/Fissures	–Ant. crud., Cistus, Graphites, Petroleum, Pix liquida.
Eyes (around)	–Chrysarobinum, Psorinum, Sulphur (see also Allergic) (also P. 52).
Face/Chin area	–Ant. crud., Borax, Cicuta vir., Dulcamara, Graphites, Hepar sulph., Mezereum, Psorinum, Silicea, Staph./strep. nosodes, Sulphur, Sulph. iod. (also p. 51)
Genital area	–Alumina, Ammon. carb., Caladium, Croton tig., Hydrastis, Picric acid, Sanicula.

Induration	–(e.g. Lick Granuloma) Calc. Fluor., Ignatia, Silicea, Tarentula cub., Thuja.
Interdigital Cysts	–Calc. sulph., Graphites, Hepar sulph. Lachesis, Silicea.
Intertrigo	–Causticum, Graphites, Hepar sulph., Petroleum, Sulphur.
Itching	–Alumen, Alumina, Ammon carb., Anacardium, Ant. crud., Arsen. alb., Bacillinum, Caladium, Calc. carb., Cistus, Dolichos, Graphites, Hypericum, Lycopodium, Mezereum, Nat. mur., Primula obcon., Psorinum, Rhus tox., Sulphur, Sulph. iod., Urtica.
Labial folds	–Ant. crud., Arsen. alb., Causticum, Clematis, Condurango, Graphites.
Mucocutaneous Junction	–Condurango, Fluor. acid., Nit. acid, Sulphur.
Nail bed	–Hepar sulph., Myristica, Sarsap, Silicea.
Nails	–Alumina, Calc. carb., Silicea, Thuja.
Red, blotchy	–Arsen. alb., Belladonna, Cistus, Hypericum, Primula obc., Ranunculus bulb., Rhus tox., Urtica.
Ringworm (and circular patches in general)	–Bacillinum, Berberis, Chrysarobinum, Sepia, Tellurium.
Rodent Ulcer	–See Mucocutaneous Junctions, also: Asterias, Calendula Lotion, Cistus can, Conium, Galium ap. ø, Hydrastis, Mercurius, Nitric acid, Sulphur (see also Mouth).
Scabs and Miliary Eczema	–Ant. crud., Calc. sulph., Dulcamara, Mezereum, Pulex, Rhus tox., Selenium (p. 80).
Scaly	–Ant. crud., Arsen alb., Nat. mur.,

	Psorinum, Rhus tox., Sulphur.
Scurf	–Arsen alb., Fluor. acid, Sepia, Sulphur, Thuja.
Sebaceous Cysts	–Baryta carb., Calc. sil., Calc. sulph., Conium, Kali iod.
Sunburn (rare)	–Cantharis, Hypericum lotion.
Tail Eczema	–Calc. fluor., Mercurius, Tarentula cub.
Thickened skin	–Hydrocotyle, Kali arsen., Sulphanilamide.
Vesicles	–Ant. crud., Rhus tox., Sulphur.
Weeping Eczema	–Cantharis, Croton tig., Graphites, Hepar sulph., Kreosotum, Mercurius, Myristica seb.
Warts	–Causticum, Nitric acid, Thuja.*

GENERAL REMEDIES:

Ichthyolum	–Is a good antiparastic remedy.
Myristica seb	–Is a good skin disinfectant.

At all times bear in mind the total patient and think in terms of a constitutional remedy where possible, also keeping in mind the general notes at the start of the chapter. (p. 49).

Nervous System

This section will not attempt to discuss the mental problems of animals since those will be covered in Chapter 12. Some conditions of the Nervous System will be found in other sections, for example, Nerve injury, Concussion and Brain injury p. 111; Disc lesions and ankylosing conditions of the spine see Locomotor p. 92; Trembling and Paralysis will be found under muscles p. 95; Eclampsia has been discussed on p. 67. Key Gaskell symdrome is on p. 120. Conditions not covered elsewhere are:

Tetanus is a specific disease of the nervous system leading to opisthotonus, lockjaw and death in severe cases! There is hypersensitivity to stimuli. The organism involved is Clostridium tetani which usually gains entrance via puncture wounds (pp. 118 and 112). Prognosis is good in the early stages.

*A great many remedies have warts in their provings.

The specific nosode should be used in conjunction with Angustura, Hypericum, Ledum, Stramonium, Strychninum or Hydrocyanic acid if there is cyanosis.

Opisthotonus without tetanus, which does occur on occasions as a result of injury or poisoning should be treated by such remedies as Cicuta, Ignatia, Nux vomica, Upas or the above, chosen according to the symptoms showing and the cause.

Chorea describes the rhythmic unusual motion of head and other parts as a result of brain damage by such agents as Distemper virus. Where a specific agent is involved, the relevant nosode should be given. Other remedies of assistance are:

Agaricus, Cicuta vir., Conium, Hyoscyamus, Mygale, Stramonium, Strychninum.

Convulsions and Fits (including Epilepsy). Epileptiform fits can take many forms (beware of heart attack differential diagnosis). Often a study of possible causes can be of more use than attempting to treat by symptoms. A paper is published in IJVH (see also p. 102 and p. 128).

Where teething may be involved — Chamomilla.
Where roundworms may be involved— Cina.
Where the animal misses its owner or— Ignatia.
member of the family or mate or a
previous home
(see Chapter 16).
Where temper seems to be involved — Nux vomica.
Where male hypersexuality— Conium.
contributes Gelsemium.
Picric acid.

Where excitability can overflow into— Ignatia,
epilepsy (see also 'excitability' later in Mag. phos,
this section) Phosphorus,
Zinc.

If fear is the cause — Aconite.

Also effective are:

Agaricus, Belladonna, Cicuta, Cocculus, Hyoscyamus, Mag. phos., Mygale, Silicea, Stramonium, Sulphur, Tarentula hisp.

As a good working standby the following should be studied carefully:

Belladonna, Chamomilla, Gelsemium, Ignatia, Silicea.

Also such nosodes as Distemperinum and Lyssin should be borne in mind.

Such poisons as Mercurius, Metaldehyde, Organophosphorus and Strychnine should also be considered as possible causes or remedies.

Hysteria and Excitability are possibly two levels of the same problem and are even likely to be less severe extensions of the problem of fits and convulsions. [see also Hyperactivity, Hysteria (p. 128)]. Consider:

Where there is anticipatory fear   – Gelsemium.
Where pain is involved   – Chamomilla.
Where bad temper is part of   – Nux vomica.
the condition
Where fever may be causing   – Belladonna.
the trouble
Where there is much restlessness   – Arsen. alb.
Where Hysteria is uppermost   – Hysocyamus.
   Stramonium.
   Veratrum album.

Passiflora, Scutellaria and Valeriana are all good 'sedating' remedies.

Loss of Balance as may happen in middle ear problems (see Ear p. 62) and brain damage, anaesthesia, etc can be helped by:

Loss of balance on shaking head   – Conium.
Where concussion is involved   – Helleborus.
Vertigo from nervousness   – Argent. nit.
With extreme sensitivity to noise   – Theridion.
As a result of heat stroke   – Glonoinium.
   Lachesis.
Vertigo of the aged animal especially   – Phosphorus.
after rest
Falls to left, head rolls from side to   – Zincum.
side, choreic movements
Falls to right   – Causticum.

CDRM is a demyelinating condition and therefore is of nervous origin. It has been treated with varying success with Causticum, Conium, Lathyrus or Plumbum met; but when advanced is not easily treated. When caught in the early stages results may be achieved in preventing development. This condition carries a very poor prognosis.

Endocrine System

The Endocrine System is a finely balanced and complex control mechanism for the reactions and metabolism of the body. The main glands were the Pituitary, Thyroid, Adrenal, Parathyroid and Pancreas (qv). Problems associated with this system should respond to correct constitutional prescribing but may also require a more specific stimulus using a potency of the appropriate glandular tissue or its hormone. Serious malfunction of the glands would require veterinary help and is beyond the scope of this book.

———

It has been stated many times in this book, simply because it is so fundamental to the principles of homoeopathy, that the foregoing pages of this chapter are a handy reference guide only. They are not, and cannot be, a full manual on the treatment of disease. Please use them freely but always with the consideration uppermost, that Homoeopathy relies for a cure on the use of the principles laid down by Hahnemann in the following steps:

a) Know your remedies (a study of Materia Medica)
b) Know the disease (a study of the Case)
c) Match a remedy to the disease in question taking all considerations into account.
And fourthly:
d) Remove obstacles to recovery.

This last step includes a consideration of environmental and nutritional factors (so vital in farm animal medicine but also of immense importance in the correct management of small animal cases) and is as important as the preceding three steps if a real cure is to be obtained. See also pp. 12/14 and Chapters 4, 5 and 6 and Appendix 8. It also includes any necessary supportive therapy.

CHAPTER 9

The Modalities

The modalities are the ways in which a symptom is affected by such factors as weather, time of day, movement, temperature, etc. These are ascertained by asking what makes it better/worse?

Aggravations (that is symptoms are made worse by)

Air – cold, dry: Aconite, Arsenicum, Bryonia, Psorinum, Rhododendron, Spongia.

Air – open: Aconite, Nux vomica.

Anger: Bryonia, Chamomilla, Nux vomica, Staphysagria.

Bright objects: Belladonna, Cantharis, Stramonium.

Cold: Aconite, Arsen alb., Bryonia, Causticum, Chamomilla, Dulcamara, Hepar Sulph., Mag. Phos., Nux vomica, Rhododendron, Rhus tox., Sepia, Silicea.

Cold Dampness: Calc. carb., Dulcamara, Mercurius, Rhus tox.

Dampness: Calc. carb., Colchicum, Dulcamara, Rhus tox.

Drinking: Arsen. alb., Cantharis, Mercurius, Rhus tox.

Excitement: Aconite, Argent nit., Coffea, Colchicum, Colocynth, Conium, Gelsemium, Hyosc., Ignatia, Nux vomica, Petroleum, Phosphorus.

Food – after: Argent nit., Arsen. alb., Bryonia, Calc. carb., Carbo. veg., Colchicum, Nux vomica, Pulsatilla, Sepia.

Fright: Aconite, Ignatia.

Jarring: Belladonna, Bryonia, Spigelia.

Light:	Belladonna, Conium, Merc. cor., Nux vomica, Phosphorus, Stramonium.
Lying down:	Arsen alb., Belladonna, Conium, Phosphorus, Pulsatilla, Rhus tox.
Movement:	Arnica, Baptisia, Belladonna, Borax, Bryonia, Cocculus, Petroleum, Phytolacca, Sanicula, Spigelia, Veratrum.
Noise:	Aconite, Belladonna, Coffea, Ignatia, Nux vomica. Theridion
Overheating:	Aconite, Ant. crud., Belladonna, Bryonia, Glonoinium, Lachesis, Nux vomica.
Pressure:	Apis, Hepar sulph., Lachesis, Merc. cor.
Rest:	Arnica, Arsen alb., Merc. sol., Pulsatilla, Rhus tox., Ruta grav., Sepia.
Lying on Side:	Belladonna, Bryonia, Causticum,
– right:	Chelidonium, Lycopodium, Mag. phos., Mercurius.
– left:	Bellis per., Colchicum, Colocynth, Lachesis, Lil. tig., Spigelia, Thuja.
Storm – before:	Bellis per., Nat. sulph., Rhododendron.
– during:	Nat. carb., Phos.
Swimming:	Ant. crud., Rhus tox., Sulphur
Time	
– in morning:	Bryonia, Calc. carb., Kali bich., Lachesis, Nat. mur., Nux vomica, Phosphorus, Pulsatilla, Sulphur.
– in afternoon:	Apis mell., Belladonna, Calc. carb., Colocynth, Hepar sulph, Lycopodium, Phosphorus, Pulsatilla.
– in evening:	Aconite, Belladonna, Bryonia, Chamomilla, Lycopodium, Mercurius, Phosphorus, Pulsatilla, Rhus. tox., Sepia.
– at night:	Aconite, Arsen alb., Belladonna, Coffea, Drosera, Lachesis, Mercurius,

| | Nit. acid, Pulsatilla, Rhus tox., Spongia, Sulphur. |
| Touch: | Aconite, Apis mel., Arnica, Belladonna, Bryonia, Chamomilla, Colchicum, Hepar sulph., Mag. phos., Nitric acid, Nux vomica, Plumbum, Silicea, Strychninum. |

Ameliorations (that is symptoms made better by)

Air -open:	Allium, Alumina, Apis, Argent nit., Cinchona, Glonoinium, Lycopodium, Nat. mur, Pulsatilla, Sepia.
Back – arching:	Colocynth, Mag. phos.
Being carried:	Chamomilla.
Cold:	Bryonia, Ledum, Phosphorus.
Cold application:	Apis, Belladonna, Phosphorus, Pulsatilla.
Cold water:	Bryonia, Phosphorus.
Consolation:	Chamomilla.
Damp weather:	Causticum.
Dark:	Euphrasia, Merc. cor.
Exercise:	Rhus tox.
Lying down:	Bryonia, Colchicum, Nat. mur., Pulsatilla.
Motion:	Alumina, Cyclamen, Dulcamara, Nitric acid, Rhus tox., Sepia.
Pressure:	Argent nit, Bryonia, Chelidonium, Colocynth, Ignatia, Mag. phos., Pulsatilla, Sepia.
Rest:	Bryonia, Colchicum, Nux vomica.
Swimming:	Causticum.
Touch:	Bryonia, Calc. carb.
Warmth:	Arsen. alb., Colocynth, Dulcamara, Hepar sulph., Ignatia, Mag. phos., Nux vom., Phos. acid, Psorinum, Rhus tox., Silicea.

All these listings are to be taken as a guide only but can prove very useful in choosing between two remedies for a particular case. The author has not verified all of them in animals but has noted down some unverified remedies according to their reputation in human treatments.

CHAPTER 10

The Generalities and First Aid

In some parts of this section little guidance will be given for choice of remedy since reference to materia medica is important. In alphabetical order:

Allergy: Such remedies as House dust and Grass pollens are indicated in conditions arising from those allergies. Galphimia glauca is a non specific anti-allergic remedy. Apis mell., Ars. alb., Astacus, Bovista, Fragaria, Primula obconica, Rhus tox. and Urtica have all been used with varied success in allergic conditions according to symptoms and cause if found.

Anaemia: Apart from standard veterinary supportive treatments consider:

Where red blood cells are damaged	– Chin Sulph. Trinitrotulene.
Where debility after long illness is the factor	– Acetic acid., China, Phos. acid.
Where malnutrition is involved	– Calc phos., Ferrum met., Silicea.
When haemorrhage has preceded it	– Acetic acid (dropsy), Arsen. alb. (restless)
When toxaemia has contributed	– Mercurius. Phosphorus.
From deficiency in Haemopoiesis	– Cuprum, Ferrum ars., Plumbum.
Haemolytic with jaundice	– Lycopodium, Phos., Merc.

Failure of clotting – Crotalus,
mechanism Lachesis, Phos.,
Secale.

Aphonia and Dysphonia (where the voice is altered):
From too much – Causticum,
barking Collinsonia.
From hysteria – Gelsemium.

Appetite (may be a symptom of serious disease, seek
veterinary advice):
Variable – Pulsatilla.
Voracious – Calc. carb., Calc.
phos., Cina,
Iodum
Increased but – Lycopodium,
quickly satisfied Sepia.
Depraved – Calc. carb., Calc.
phos., Cina.,
Phosphorus.

Bites (cat or dog): Arnica, Hepar sulph, Calendula lotion.
Depending upon which site is injured
veterinary attention should be sought.
Bites and Stings Apis, Cantharis, Hypericum, Ledum,
(from insects): Urtica, Hypericum/Calendula lotion
or Arnica lotion.
Bites (from snake): Cedron, Echinacea – seek urgent
veterinary attention.
Burns/Scalds: Apis mell., Cantharis, Urtica, in-
fected: Hepar sulph.
Collapse: Carbo veg., Camphora, Laurocerasus
Ø, seek urgent veterinary attention.
Convalescence: Acetic acid, Calc. carb., Calc. phos.,
China, Ferrum phos., Kali carb.,
Lecithin, Phos. acid.
Dehydration: China, Phos. acid. (seek veterinary
advice).
Fever: Aconite, Belladonna, China, Chin.
sulph., Echinacea, Gelsemium,
Pulsatilla, Pyrogen, Sulphur (veter-
inary attention may be necessary).
Frost Bite: Agaricus. If followed by:

Gangrene: Carbo veg., Echinacea, Lachesis, Secale, seek veterinary attention.

Haemorrhage: Treat homoeopathically according to the character of the blood and bleeding. Veterinary attention should be sought if any quantity of blood is being lost. See also post operative problems.

From trauma	– Arnica, Millefolium.
With coldness, convulsions etc.	– China.
Bright red	– Aconite, Ipecacuanha, Millefolium, Nitric acid.
Clotting with bright fluid	– Ferrum, Sabina.
Clotting dark	– Elaps, Hamamelis Thlaspi.
Watery, dark, decomposing	– Crotalus, Lachesis, Secale.
Watery, bright	– Phosphorus.
Heavy breathing	– Ipecacuanha.
Anxiety	– Aconite.
Collapse	– Carbo veg.
Active haemorrhage, bright red	– Nitric Acid.
Post operative seepage	– Strontia.
Post partum, red flow	– Nitric acid, Sabina.
Post partum, builds up then gushes	– Ipecacuanha.
Post partum, continual, dark	– Secale.
After haemorrhage consider	– Acetic acid, Arsen. alb., Phos. acid., Strontia.

Heat Stroke:	Belladonna, Gelsemium, Glonoinium, Sulphur.	
Hypersexuality:	Camphor, Conium, Lyssin, Picric acid, Pulsatilla (see also pp. 78, 81, 128)	

Ill Effects of (see also Never Well Since):

Abortion	– Kali carb.
Anaesthetic	– See post operative problems.

Anxiety/Apprehension leading to:

Diarrhoea	– Arg. nit.
Incontinence	– Gelsemium.
Restlessness	– Arsen alb.
Near paralysis	– Gelsemium.
Stupor	– Opium.
Autumn changeable weather	– Dulcamara.
Chilling (p. 125)	– Aconite.
Cold and Damp weather	– Rhus tox., Dulcamara.
Cold, dry weather	– Aconite, Rhododendron.
Excitement	– Argent nit., Coffea, Gelsemium.
Grief	– Ignatia, Nat. mur., Phos. acid.
Haemorrhage.	– see Haemorrhage
Heat	– Glonoinium, Sulphur.
Illness	– see Convalescence.
Injury	– Arnica.
Over exertion	– Arnica, Phos. acid.
Over eating	– Nux vomica.
Parturition	– Caulophyllum, Pulsatilla, Sabina, Sepia (see also Female p. 83).
Rotten food	– Arsen alb., Camphor, Pyrogen,

	Veratrum album.
Shock	– Aconite, Arnica.
Specific diseases	– See 'Never Well Since' p. 113 and Specific Diseases p. 117.
Surgery	– See Post Operative Problems p. 113.
Vaccination	– Ant tart., Lachesis, Silicea, Thuja. (also p. 139)
Injury:	Always Arnica then think of:
Adhesions	– Calc. fluor., Silicea.
Bone	– Ruta grav., Symphytum.
Brain/Head	– Baryta carb., Cicuta, Helleborus, Nat. sulph.
Bruising	– Arnica, Bellis per., Hamamelis.
Concussion	– Helleborus, Nat. sulph.
Cornea	– Ledum, Merc. corr.
Extremities	– Hypericum (rich in nerve endings).
Graze	– Arnica, Hypericum/ Calendula lotion.
Joints/Fibrous tissue	– Rhus tox., Ruta grav.
Orbital area	– Symphytum.
Periosteum	– Ruta grav.
Scar tissue breaking open	– Causticum.
With Shock/ Fright	– Aconite.
Sphincters	– Staphysagria.
Spinal	– Helleborus, Hypericum.

111

Deep Tissues (Esp Pelvic) Wounds:	– Bellis Per.
Bleeding:	– Phos., Strontia.
Cuts:	– Staphysagria, Calendula lotion.
Granulation: (exuberant)	– Nitric acid, Silicea, Thuja.
Haematoma (ear):	– Arnica, Hamamelis.
Infected:	– Hepar sulph., Calendula lotion.
Laceration:	– Arnica, Calendula lotion
Old injuries: (won't heal)	– Calc. sulph., Causticum.
Puncture:	– Ledum.
Scar tissue:	– Calc. fluor., Graphites, Sil., Thuja, Thiosin.
Ulcerated/ Ungranulated:	– Arsen alb., Galium aparine Ø.

Neoplasia: See also footnote★

Any Malignancy	– Arsen alb., Viscum alb
Abdominal	– Hydrastis.
Bony	– See Skeletal System p. 90, Calc. fl., Hekla Lava.
Lipoma	– Baryta Carb., Thuja.
Lymphatic	– See Lymphatic p.89.
Mammary	– See Female p. 86.
Stomach	– Hydrastis Ornithogallum Ø. See Digestive System p. 68.
Ulcerated	– Asterias.

★ *Neoplasia has been treated with Iscador ® therapy with varying results. More work needs to be done on this to increase predictability of results.*

Warts   – See Skin p. 100.
Always pay special attention to diet in cases of neoplasia.

'Never well since . . .': This is in quotation marks since it is a common saying of both human patients and pet owners during history taking. It means what it says and can be followed by any of life's events (illness, specific disease, pregnancy, parturition, birth, oestrus, poisoning, vaccination, injury etc). When such a sentence appears in the history one should not ignore it, it can be the key to the successful treatment of the case. Treat such historical comments as if they were part of the present symptoms and surprising results can follow. See Chapter 16 – Case Histories for examples.
See also pp. 110, 36.

Nystagmus: Agaricus, Cicuta, Gelsemium, Physostigma, according to concomitant symptoms.

Obesity: This is not really a disease state but can be helped by a) Male and Female treatment as in relevant sections, if applicable. b) Calc. carb., Capsicum, Graphites, Kali carb., according to symptoms, also Phytolacca Berry tincture.

Photophobia: Aconite, Argent nit., Belladonna, Euphrasia, Mercurius, Rhus tox. according to concomitant symptoms.

Post Operative Problems:

Adhesions	– Acetic acid, Calc. fl.
Anaesthetic problems	– potentised Anaesthetic, Acetic acid, Opium
Bladder surgery	– Staphysagria
Bleeding	– Strontia (and see Haemorrhage).

Bone Surgery	– Symphytum, Ruta grav.
Bruising	– Arnica, or (deep bruising) Bellis per.
Constipation	– Nux vomica.
Convalescence help	– Phos. acid, Phosphorus, Kali phos.
Dental surgery	– Arnica, Hypericum, Ruta grav.
Eye surgery	– Senega, Symphytum.
Fear	– Aconite.
Gassy Colic	– China, Colocynth, Raphanus.
Intestinal Stasis	– Carbo veg., Nux vomica, Opium.
Joints	– Rhus tox., Ruta grav.
Oedema	– Apis mell.
Pain	– Unwilling to move a muscle: Bryonia.
	– general pain symptoms: Hypericum.
	– irritable pain: Chamomilla.
Recovery, slow, languid and shivery	– Kali sil.
Renal Colic	– Berberis.
Sepsis	– Hepar sulph., Pyrogen (see below).
Shock (qv)	– Camphor, Strontia, Veratrum album.
Soreness around wound	– Rhus tox., Staphysagria.

| | Vomiting | – Ipecacuanha, Nux vomica, Phosphorus, Staphysagria. |

Always remember Arnica and Calendula wherever possible.

Pre Operative: Aconite, Argent nit. or Gelsemium for the anxiety and fear (see pp. 127/128).

	Bronchial problems	– Antimonium tart.
	Bruising preventive	– Arnica.
	Heart therapy	– See p. 88.

Sepsis and Abscess:

	Acute	– Hepar sulph., Myristica sebifera.
	Chronic	– Calc. sulph., Silicea.
	Dental Abscess	– Merc. sol.
	Embedded foreign body	– Silicea.
	With local purpling	– Lachesis, Tarentula.
	With Septicaemia	– Arsen alb., Echinacca, Pyrogen.
	With Toxaemia	– Arsen alb., Echinacea, Pyrogen.

Hepar sulph. and Merc. sol. both abort suppuration in high potency and encourage it in low potency.

Shock: Aconite, Arnica, Camphor, Nat. mur., Veratrum album. See also Post Operative p. 113. (Bach Rescue Remedy, although not Homoeopathy, merits inclusion here).

Sleepless: Apis mell., Arsen alb., Chamomilla, Coffea, Nux vom., Pulsatilla, Scutellaria.

Terminal Illness: To ease the sufferings prior to

euthanasia – Arsen alb.,
if actually dying – Tarentula cubensis.

Thirst: Increased: – Aconite, Arsen alb., Bryonia, Calc. carb., Capsicum, Chamomilla, China, Lycopodium, Mercurius, Nat. mur., Rhus tox., Veratrum album.
Increased thirst can herald serious disease so consult a veterinary surgeon.

Decreased: – Apis mell., Carbo veg, Gelsemium, Ignatia, Pulsatilla, Sabadilla.

Vaccinosis: See Chapter 15 and p. 111

Weight Loss: Acetic acid, Calc. phos., Glycerinum, Hydrastis, Iodum, Lecithin, Phos. acid, Silicea, Thuja. Seek veterinary advice since unexplained weight loss can be a sign of serious disease.

Worms: See p. 68

Yawning: Aconite, Chelidonium, Cocculus, Graphites, Ignatia, Lycopodium, Merc. corr., Platina, Sulphur. This symptom often appears in a history taking and can, on occasions, be useful to help guide one to a remedy.

CHAPTER II

Specific Diseases

See also Chapter 14 – PREVENTION.

Dogs

Parvovirus Disease. This is a disease of repeated vomiting with bloody dysentery. Rapid dehydration follows and death is very likely if treatment is ineffective.

Aconite as always is given in the very early stages.

Apormorphine, Arsen. alb., Phosphorus or Veratrum album are very useful to slow down or prevent the vomiting and diarrhoea. Baptisia has also been used on occasions. Be guided by presenting symptoms.

It is important to prevent the dehydration both during and after the acute phase and here China or Phos. acid can be a great help in addition to fluid therapy. The nosode should also be given later as in all specific diseases, to aid recovery.

Distemper/Hard Pad: This disease is not as common as it once was although in urban areas, where vaccination has not been universally accepted, it is still seen. It is a virus disease affecting all parts of the body including Nervous System, Digestive System, Eyes, Chest and Skin. The Nose and Pads are frequently affected.

Aconite should be given, as usual, in the early febrile stages. The various symptoms, as they appear, should be treated according to the similia principle from knowledge of the materia medica. The sections on Eyes, Nervous system, etc in Chapter 8 should be a guide to useful remedies.

Graphites, Antimonium crud., Nitric acid and Thuja should be considered to help the involvement of the pads and nose. The nosode given later will help recovery.

Leptospirosis: This is a name encompassing disease caused by Leptospira icterohaemorrhagiae, which is associated mainly with liver disease and jaundice and Leptospira canicola which is associated mostly with kidney disease. The orthodox vaccination and proprietary homoeopathic Leptospira nosode cover against both organisms.

In the case of liver disease, Phosphorus, Chelidonium, Berberis, Arsen. alb., Lycopodium, Mercurial remedies and Carduus mar. should all be considered. Aconite should be given in the acute phase.

In the case of kidney involvement think of Arsen. alb., Berberis, Baptisia, Phosphorus, Mercurius, Plumbum and Kali chlor. (see Kidneys).

The combined nosode should be used later in either case and continued after an apparent cure to lessen the risk of 'carrier' status in surviving patients.

Hepatitis or Rubarth's Disease: This is rarely seen nowadays as a result of widespread conventional vaccination. It is a virus disease affecting mainly the liver but also all other parts of the body since the virus is a virulent one. All mucuous membranes are affected and kidney involvement gives rise to spread of disease. Coagulability of the blood is adversely affected and the eyes may become cloudy.

Aconite in the acute phase, as in all acute pyrexias, can be very beneficial. One then has to prescribe according to the prevalent symptoms at the time. See Throat, Mouth, Eyes, Liver, Kidneys and Haemorrhage for further details. In conjunction with symptomatic prescribing one should use the Adenovirus nosode later to aid recovery and reduce the usually lengthy convalescent period.

Tetanus or Lockjaw: Arises from the toxin of the bacteria Clostridium tetani interfering with the neuromuscular junction. The result is an overstimulation of the muscles all over the body giving symptoms of jerking, hyperaesthesia, locked jaw (whence its name) and opisthotonus. The organism involved is anaerobic and favours puncture wounds for its proliferation. Hence the value of Ledum after puncture wounds. See Nervous System for treatments (p. 100). [Conventional vaccine is not routine.]

Kennel Cough: This is probably caused by several organisms among which is Bordetella. It is an upper respiratory tract infection but can rarely affect the lungs. It gains its name from the fact that it is able to spread most easily in boarding kennels where dogs are grouped together so is most often seen after the summer holiday when a dog returns from boarding. Prevention is by use of the nosode and treatment is according to the guidelines on Coughs in Chapter 8. It is usually not a serious disease but can be very troublesome and annoying both to dog and owner since the noise of the cough is very harsh and repeated frequently. Conventional vaccine is not routine (IJVH Vol. 2 No. 1, p. 45 and follow-up in Vol. 2 No. 2, p. 57).

Cats

Panleucopaenia also known as Feline Enteritis and (mistakenly) as Cat Flu (see later): This is highly contagious and often fatal. Orthodox vaccination has reduced its incidence to a great extent but it is still seen in kittens and unvaccinated cats. Fever, (where Aconite, as usual in the acute phase, can be useful) diarrhoea and severe dehydration characterise the disease.

Arsenicum, China, Echinacea, Mercurius and Phos. acid can all be of value depending on the symptoms (see Diarrhoea, etc.). Therapy in the form of fluid infusion is of great value also and should not be forgotten. Readers should be reminded not to forget, when embarking on homoeopathy, the value of good, sound nursing and supportive therapy. Also remember the nosode later.

Cat Flu or Feline Influenza: As in the human, is a complex condition associated with many viruses and secondary bacteria. Conventional vaccination may be of help but often viruses not included in the vaccine package can be involved. The nosode or even a specific nosode for the outbreak, can be of great value and symptomatic treatment is invaluable. See Nose, Eyes, Throat, Sinuses etc. Dehydration may also play a part so remember Phos. acid or China and conventional fluid therapy.

Feline Infectious Anaemia: Is a malaria like disease of the red blood cells (an over simplified description). As with all infectious diseases, early fever can be helped with Aconite and a nosode could be used. Anaemia is the strong feature of the disease more than the febrile signs and here one should consider all remedies which are of help with anaemia, taking into account the concomitant symptoms (see

Anaemia p. 107). Remember supportive therapy, nutrition and vitamin and mineral treatment to aid recovery and blood regeneration.

Feline Infectious Peritonitis: This is an obscure viral disease causing gradual but extreme swelling of the abdomen with straw coloured fluid. Inappetance, jaundice, dyspnoea and weight loss can all be present. There are often white flecks in the abdominal fluid and white deposits on the peritoneal lining. Use of the nosode will aid the recovery and elimination of virus. Symptomatic treatment such as Acetic acid, Apis mell., Blatta amer., Helleborous, Lycopodium and Senecio are worth pursuing but the outlook not good. Again, supportive treatment in the form of fluids etc. is essential. A nosode is available.

Feline Leukaemia: This is a virus disease of the bone marrow, lymph nodes, lymphatic system in general, kidneys, immune system and haemopoietic system. Some cats may successfully recover but the outlook is not good, supportive therapy, possible nosode therapy and symptomatic treatment are, again, the lines of treatment as in all infectious diseases (see also Lymphatic System p. 89 for remedies which may help). Similarly with FIV.

Key Gaskell Syndrome (Feline Dysautonomia): Is a disease of unknown aetiology at present and very recent incidence. It is included in this section on specific diseases (where one would expect to find diseases as a result of infection with specific organisms) because it has caused a lot of worry and much mortality in the few years since it has been recognised. The outlook is not good but there are quite a number of successful recoveries usually as a result of painstaking supportive therapy and nursing. As its alternative name suggests it is a disease affecting the autonomic nervous system. It is characterised by dilated pupils of the eye, dry mouth, malfunctioning bowels, difficulty in swallowing and gross dehydration. Supportive therapy is vital but several homoeopathic remedies exist which can be of help. Here again one has to choose between them on the basis of symptom matching (the similia principle).

Belladonna, Calc. carb., Gelsemium, Hyoscyamus, Nux moschata and Stramonium are the ones that spring to mind most readily. One must consider primarily the mental disposition, as far as it can be determined, in prescribing a remedy but also take into account bowel function, abdominal distension, vomiting, etc. where signs are present. Other remedies used include Alumina, Collinsonia, Lobelia, Nicotine, Neostigmine and Wyethia (see also p. 59).

Salmonellosis: Can affect cats, guinea pigs, rabbits and mice and is usually characterised by a septicaemia and enteritis (often bleeding) resulting in very rapid death. It is preventable by the use of the nosode and Baptisia has a reputation in the control and cure of Salmonella disease. Treatment by nosode, Baptisia and appropriate similia should be successful if caught in time. Here, again, appropriate use of antibiotic may 'buy' time if in doubt.

Rabbits

Myxomatosis: Is a virus induced disease transmitted by the rabbit flea from the wild rabbit population. There is an orthodox vaccine available and there is also a homoeopathic nosode as in the case of most specific diseases. This disease is characterised by a swollen head and neck (gelatinous tumours and fluid collect beneath the skin) purulent ocular discharge, loss of appetite, weakness and eventually death follow. Prevention is the key to this disease by use of the nosode. Treatment is usually unsuccessful, the domestic rabbit being particularly susceptible. One should consider Acetic acid, Abrotanum and Mercurius sol. for example along with supportive therapy but the humanitarian justifications of persisting with a rabbit which is so ill with a poor prognosis are doubtful.

This discussion of a rabbit disease conveniently leads us on to a consideration of the particular problems to be found in the **smaller pets such as rabbits, rodents and birds**. It is essential to remember several points in connection with these species. Firstly, and this applies especially to the very small species, they do not tolerate rough handling and unless they are accustomed to handling by their owner, even the minimum can upset them badly*. Secondly, they are also

---

* *Treat as for shock p. 115.*

very susceptible to **hypothermia**[†], especially when ill, and care should be taken to ensure that this is not a problem. Thirdly, there are a number of idosyncratic responses to antibiotic therapy which makes homoeopathy a very acceptable mode of treatment. Such idiosyncracies are summarised by the following fatal incompatibilities:—

Guinea Pigs	— Penicillin, Streptomycin and Erythromycin.
Hamsters	— Penicillin, Streptomycin.
Birds	— Streptomycin, Procaine Penicillin.

Fourthly, the nutrient requirements of these pets vary greatly and great care should be taken to ensure the correct diet for the species. Advice should be sought on this subject from someone experienced in the particular species. For example Guinea Pigs require Vitamin C in their diet.

Fifthly, the management of each species is very important and should be related to its own special biology. Care should be taken to seek advice on this subject too.

Where specific problems are covered in this text, reference to remedies should be used as a guide only. There is no substitute for homoeopathic prescribing by first principles. Bearing in mind the difficulties and dangers involved in handling some of these species it is worth noting that homoeopathic remedies can be administered via the drinking water if the animal is not too ill to drink. There will be no mention of **fish diseases** here since the author has no experience of treating fish diseases homoeopathically[‡]. The usual principles should apply, however, and remedies can be given in the water direct. When in any doubt with regard to the treatment of these species, consult a veterinary surgeon.

Diarrhoea in the Rabbit: Is not a specific disease but it is worth considering here as a special subject. Often it can result from changes of diet, chilling, shock, milk feeding (rabbits unfortunately do like milk but it is a wholly unsuitable food) and it can also result from overenthusiastic

---

[†] *See Chilling p. 110 and p. 125*
[‡] *Since the appearance of the 1st Edition the author has had the good fortune to treat many fish problems (both domestic and farm). There is a small section on the treatment of tortoises, snakes, lizards and fish in Appendix 10 (p. 188)*

cleaning out of the droppings. In order to digest cellulose sufficiently some of the food passes twice through the digestive system and the rabbit produces two kinds of pellet. The crumbly pale green ones are those which have been through once and the dark shiny ones are the final product. The rabbit must be given access to the first stage droppings or digestive disorders can result and often a vitamin deficiency too, unless the diet has been formulated to obviate the need for this. Should diarrhoea occur the treatment according to symptoms is important but consider especially Colchicum and Mercurius. (Coccidiososis is a particularly virulent form of diarrhoea). One should consider also China or Phos. acid. Reference to major diarrhoea remedies however is preferable to just picking on one or two likely remedies from this page (see p. 72 *et seq*).

Conjunctivitis and Rhinitis: Are not uncommon where many rabbits are kept together but here no special considerations apply to the rabbit, refer to the pages on Eyes and Nose in Chapter 8.

Loss of Balance: Is relatively common in the domestic rabbit and usually results from an ear infection. Consider Conium, Hepar sulph. and Merc. sol. as homoeopathic treatments and if ear mites are involved the infestation should be removed. (see p. 61 and 62).

Salmonella: See Cats (p. 121).

Guinea Pigs

Are very prone to skin disorders usually resulting from a deficiency of vitamin C but also a result of mange infection. Consider any symptomatically chosen remedy but remember especially Ant. crud., Graphites, Muriatic acid, Nat. mur., Phosphorus, Psorinum, Sulphur and Zincum met.

Diarrhoea can also affect guinea pigs as in all other species and the remedies one should choose will be decided by the same factors.

Salmonella: See Cats (p. 121).

Hamsters

Dermatitis: Occurs in hamsters as in other species and choosing a remedy by symptoms is again the only way in which one can function. An exception to this would be the use of Ignatia or Aconite should the appropriate circumstances have occured to initiate the mental processes of bereavement or shock to which these little creatures can be especially prone. Remember Rescue Remedy too.

Wet Tail: In hamsters is not a specific disease but describes the appearance of the animal with diarrhoea. Choose appropriate remedies by the usual homoeopathic means. The expected survival time of one of these tiny creatures when affected with diarrhoea is minimal so prompt action and good nursing are essential. (See p. 72.)

Rats and Mice

Suffer few diseases that are worthy of special mention but one which is worthy of a few lines is **Ringtail** in rats. Should the temperature and humidity in the environment be hostile, a disturbance of the circulation of the tail occurs and annular constrictions appear. The tail can drop off. A remedy which should be particularly effective here is Secale. Sadly though, once the condition has been noticed it is often too late to prevent the consequences. For other problems the general discussions on other species apply.

Birds

By far the most common problem of birds brought to the veterinary surgeon is **injury**. Arnica, Rhus tox., Ruta grav. and Symphytum are all equally valuable to birds as they are to mammals. **Fracture** healing is aided by Symphytum, bruising is reduced by Arnica etc. Remember Rescue Remedy.

Aconite, Hepar sulph. and Hypericum are also used in their usual contexts and Secale can be of especial use in toe and wing injuries as circulation so often suffers. Calendula lotion is also of its customary value so it is worth remembering homoeopathy can form as useful a form of first aid and continuing treatment in birds as in mammals.

Diarrhoea: See p. 72.

Mange: Sulphur is very useful and in the particular problem of the budgerigar of mange around the cere consider in addition, Nitric acid, Silicea or Thuja, with Hypericum/Calendula Lotion.

Eyes: No special notes, see section on Eyes p. 52.

Eggbound: Consider as a first treatment, Caulophyllum and Sepia. Use Arnica.

Newcastle Disease, Paramyxo virus and Salmonellosis and other specific diseases should all be preventable by judicious use of the relevant nosode or treatable by the nosode and relevant symptomatic prescribing as in the previous chapters. The author has no experience of these specific problems but sees no reason why the usual principles should not apply. Remember any Ministry regulations. In the particular case of **Frounce** in pigeons consider Graphites, Nitric acid or Rhus tox.

Feather Pecking: This very often results from mental disturbance (see p. 127). Consider also Sepia, Thallium, Folliculinum, Sulphur.

Chilling: Aconite, Calc. carb., Calc. phos., Dulcamara, Rhus tox., Silicea. (See also p. 110).

Inevitably the author's experience with all the 'exotic' species of pets is smaller than that with cats and dogs but results have been very encouraging and the foregoing pages should act as a guide to those intending to try homoeopathy on them. As always with homoeopathy one can be assured of no harmful consequences arising out of its use so long as, while trying to improve one's skills in the field of homoeopathy, one is not neglecting a perfectly good orthodox treatment or essential nursing procedure to the detriment of the patient.

CHAPTER 12

Mental Problems

The scope of this book, and the obvious problems concerned with discerning mental symptoms in animals, precludes me from making this a lengthy chapter. Suffice to say that mental disorders most definitely do occur in pet animals and that one can sometimes discern them from the symptoms shown and sometimes only divine them from circumstance. Many of the symptoms of such disorder are subjective and therefore locked within the patient, never to be observed by us. Some are objective, that is one can perceive them. It is the observation of these symptoms which is of first importance, one has to evaluate them and then one has to deduce what is the mental process governing them. It is at this stage that one can come adrift but it is always worth making the effort.

Mental problems can usefully be divided into three categories:–

1 Those whose symptoms are easily perceived from which one can relatively certainly deduce the underlying mental cause.

2 Those whose symptoms are not easily seen but the patient's demeanour betrays a mental problem whose nature may be very difficult to define.

3 Those whose symptoms appear as an entirely different manifestation in another organ eg the skin or digestive system, and therefore lead one to ignore the underlying mental cause, unsuccessfully attacking the visible clinical problem.

Go back to Hahnemann to remind yourself of the importance of all mental symptoms (he did have the advantage of access to subjective symptoms) Paras 210–213 inclusive, of Hahnemann's Organon draw one's attention to this con-

cept. Refer to British Homoeopathic Journal Volume 73
No 3 July 1983 page 165 for discussion of this problem
when dealing with animals.

Demeanour and disposition will, of course, at all times
affect one's choice of remedy in illness, especially in a
constitutional context. However, there follows a list of
remedies often associated with certain mental processes and
it can act as a good guide in treating cases where one
considers mental problems to be the major problem. The
indications can also act as a guide to selection of a
constitutional remedy. Remember also the importance of
treating historical problems (see p. 113 under 'Never Well
Since') because an incident can leave a mental mark which
can persist for a lifetime.

Aggression	– Belladonna, Nux vomica.
Anger	– Chamomilla, Colocynth, Crocus, Hepar sulph., Nux vomica.
Anxiety/ Apprehension	– Argent nit., Gelsemium, Lycopodium.
Aversions to:	
Being left	– Capsicum, Ignatia, Phos., Phos. acid, Pulsatilla. (see also Bereavement/ Loneliness and fear of solitude.)
Heat	– Sulphur.
Veterinary premises	– Silicea.
Bereavement/ Loneliness	– Aurum, Ignatia, Phos. acid, Psorinum, Pulsatilla. (See also Aversion to being left and fear of solitude.)
Boredom	– Argent nit., Arsen. alb., Lilium tigrinum (Boredom can lead to aimless activity including self–mutilation. See p. 98 Lick granuloma & p. 125.
Desires:	
Cold Water	– Arsen. alb., Bryonia, Mercury.
Company	– Argent nit., Arsen. alb., Lycopodium, Phosphorus.

Consolation/ Reassurance	– Chamomilla, Pulsatilla.
Cool	– Sulphur.
Fresh Air	– Apis.
Heat	– Arsenicum, Psorinum.
Depraved appetite	– Calc. carb., Calc. phos., Cicuta, Cina, Cinchona, Cobaltum, Phosphorus.
Excitability	– Belladonna, Hyoscyamus, Mag. phos., Stramonium.
Fear/Fright/Shock	– Aconite, Nat. mur.
Fear of:	
Being Carried	– Borax, Sanicula.
Car	– Borax, Bryonia, Cocculus, Gelsemium, Sanicula.
Dark	– Phosphorus, Stramonium
Forthcoming ordeal	– Argent nit., Gels., Lycopodium, Silicea.
Motion	– Bryonia.
Noise	– Nux vom., Phosphorus.
Solitude	– Hyosc., Kali carb., Lycopodium, Phos., Stramonium. (See also Aversion to being left and Bereavement/Loneliness.)
Touch	– Arnica, Chamomilla, Lachesis, Nux vom., Plumbum (abdomen).
Thunder	– Aconite, Gels, Hyosc, Nat carb, Phos., Rhododendron.
Hyperactivity	– Arsen alb., Coffea, Ignatia. (See also Excitability, Hysteria, Fits.)
Hypersexuality	– Cantharis, Ferula, Gels., Hyosc., Origanum, Phos., Picric acid, Tarent hisp. (see also Sexual Systems. and p. 111)
Hysteria	– Gels., Hyosc., Ignatia, Tarent hisp., Valeriana. (see also Fits, p. 101/2 Excitability, Hyperactivity.)
Indifference	– Platina, Sepia
Irritability	– Capsicum, Chamomilla, Cina, Crocus, Nux vom., Sepia.
Jealousy	– Apis mell, Lachesis
Obstinacy	– Silicea, Sulphur, Tub. bov.
Panic	– Gels., Phos., Stramonium.

Rage	– Hyoscyamus.
Resentment	– Lachesis, Staphysagria.
Restlessness/	– Aconite, Arsen alb., Chamomilla,
Fidgeting	Coffea, Ignatia, Rhus tox.,
	Stramonium.
Roaming tendency	– Bryonia, Veratrum alb. (see also
	Hypersexuality.)
Shyness/Timidity	– Baryta carb., Ignatia, Pulsatilla,
	Sulphur.

In all cases these suggestions can only be taken as a guide but these remedies prove very useful, for their stated indications, a great many times.

CHAPTER 13

Special Problems of the Young and Old

Problems common in the adolescent male and female have been discussed at length under the heading of the Male and Female Sexual Systems – Chapter 8. It is worth considering separately however the particular problems of the very young and very old cat or dog to help bring what is written in earlier chapters into a practical context.

Puppies/Kittens Through to Puberty

Proper attention to the mother before, during and after the birth process is essential to the offspring's well being. Apart from all the benefit of proper nursing and management, study again the homoeopathic treatments outlined on p. 83 *et seq.* which have a particular benefit at this time. As for the offspring themselves, the results of a *traumatic birth* can be minimised with the use of Arnica (bruising), Baryta carb. and Nat. sulph. (brain damage), Laurocerasus (cyanosis) and Aspidosperma (respiratory failure) see also p. 84. Avoid all use of drugs in pregnancy.

In the *suckling period* various problems can show themselves. *'Fading puppies'* is a condition manifesting itself in progressive loss of weight, strength and body temperature in newborn pups up to about three weeks of age. Hepatitis virus, Herpes virus, Escherichia coli and many other infective agents have the power to cause this problem. The progressive weakness leads to inability to suck and, commonly, death. There may or may not be diarrhoea. This condition is usually not encountered in the occasionally bred dam on its own in a household but more commonly in larger breeding establishments where reservoirs of infection are built up. If the specific agent involved is known then preventive measures during pregnancy and at birth should be adopted using the relevant homoeopathic nosode. Aconite in the early stages, Arsenicum album, if vomiting and diarrhoea are present, Carbo veg. if pups are cold and collapsed and Abrotanum if the navel is weeping. Calc. phos., China, Echinacea and Phos. acid can all be of use according to the symptoms. The puppies should also be kept warm and dry with clean bedding. A hot water bottle insulated by three or four layers of towel is a good form of heating. Supportive fluid therapy is valuable.

Diarrhoea in the very young should be treated according to symptoms as in all animals (see p. 72).

Kittens can get very *gummed up eyes* with cat flu virus infection and here the nosode can be of great use (as also in preventing the condition) in conjunction with such remedies as Argent nit., Graphites and Pulsatilla.

At a few days of age *dew claws* are removed from puppies and in some breeds tails are still *docked*. Aconite, Arnica and Staphysagria are worth remembering for troubles at this stage.

When it comes to *weaning time*, Ignatia can prove useful for both dam and offspring, as too can Phos acid, particularly if diarrhoea ensues. Both before and after weaning, pups can suffer from colic and even fits as a result of *round worm* infection. Here Cina can be of tremendous value. P. 68.

Next, is the period of *fast growth* particularly for puppies and here Calc phos. should be remembered for adequate bone growth. One dose weekly for one or two months as a routine can be very beneficial*. Diarrhoea and Colic can be fairly common during the growing phase and should be treated according to symptoms (see Diarrhoea p. 72. Colic p. 69).

Teething can also cause many problems in this period and Chamomilla should always be borne in mind. Many cases of epileptiform fits arise from teething troubles and Chamomilla can stop these quite readily, but teething can cause many unrelated problems such as sore eyes, colic and diarrhoea too. Even some really bad chewers can be stopped with Chamomilla.

Intussusception, Hiccough, Foreign Body swallowing and *Travel Sickness* primarily occur in the young and growing

---

* See also pp. 90 and 37.

pet and should be treated according to p. 69, 68 and 68 respectively.

Congenital Heart problems and joint troubles also manifest themselves as the animal gains in weight and is moving towards full growth (these problems are dealt with on pages 88 *et seq.* and 90 *et seq.*). Entropion also manifests itself as the puppy grows and a discussion of this problem is to be found on p. 54.

Vaccination usually is carried out at about three to four months if conventional vaccine is used and this is not to be lightly decried since it has saved countless dogs from terrible effects of Distemper, Hepatitis, Parvovirus and Leptospirosis. Homoeopathic prevention of these diseases by the nosode can be instituted at an earlier age however as also for Enteritis and Flu for kittens (see chapters 11, 14). Many use the nosode alone, but they can be used alongside conventional vaccination. Should any harmful effects of conventional vaccine be experienced, the relevant nosodes should be given along with Thuja. On occasions too, the adjuvant portion of a killed vaccine can cause trouble (e.g. Aluminium Hydroxide) whereupon the potentised form of this can be given with great effect, reducing the local pain and risk of abscessation. (See also p. 141 for a discussion of the problems associated with vaccination).

Towards the end of the growing period in dogs, puberty starts to show itself and this can result in many problems. These are dealt with under Male and Female Sexual Systems.

Careful nutrition is vital in pregnancy and the growing period.

The Old Dog/Cat

They have particular problems as do the youngsters. In this section I shall draw attention to them and refer to the text in other parts of this book for detail. Old age should not be considered a disease, the aged should be allowed to spend the evening of their lives healthy, if possible, and to die healthy.

Leg Problems: All arthritic and rheumatic complaints become magnified in the older animal but respond in a very dramatic way to correct homoeopathic prescribing. The leg weakness of the German Shepherd responds to Conium in its early stages (although the symptom is not confined to that breed†). The pain of Hip Dysplasia can be helped greatly by Colocynth along with other rheumatic/arthritic remedies described on p. 93 *et seq.*

Growths: Are more prevalent on older animals especially dogs and some can respond well (see p. 112).

The *Heart, Kidneys and Eyes* are also prone to greater problems in the older patient but the treatment for these is adequately covered in the relevant pages of this book, that is, p. 88, 76 and 52 respectively.

Ageing in general can produce loss of hair (consider Thallium), deafness loss of elasticity in the tissue in general and progressive weakness; consider Agnus castus, Argent nit., Causticum, Conium, Lycopodium, Silicea and Thiosinaminum. Sometimes these processes can be slowed and complaints arising from such processes can be improved markedly. A good diet is vital.

Collapsed animals and *terminal* patients can also be helped by appropriate remedies, apart from helping the heart as necessary. Reference to pages 108 and 116 can give encouraging results. In terminal disease the eventual duty of euthanasia must not be shirked when circumstances demand.

Ageing dogs often are *restless* at night causing themselves and their owners great disturbance. Coffea or Arsen. alb. have proved useful in these circumstances.

One should not start out by believing that an old dog or cat can be rejuvenated, ageing processes reversed or terminal illness suddenly evaporated by the use of homoeopathy in the aged but its results should not be ignored. One should not deprive the aged pet of such beneficial, gentle and easy remedies as can apply to their special case, for these remedies can, if not add on years (and in some cases they do this) to the animal's life, most certainly improve the quality of life left to such dignified creatures. The aged must not be deprived of their dignity by relentless illness.

† *See CDRM p. 103.*

CHAPTER 14

Homoeopathy in the Prevention of Disease

A system of medicine which does not recognise the need for prevention of disease is a non-starter to the sound minded observer. Homoeopathy not only recognises it but it has an unrivalled ability, in certain fields, to prevent disease.

Canine Parvovirus has the unenviable position of being the most notorious dog disease at present and is being very well contained by conventional vaccination but only animals over fourteen weeks of age can be vaccinated with any guarantee of success*. Even these can break down. Younger puppies are a real problem. The nosode prepared from Parvovirus, however, can give us very real protection in any age of dog (see Chapter 11 on Specific Disease).

Nosodes can be prepared from Distemper, Leptospirosis, Hepatitis, Feline Enteritis, Cat Flu, Staphylococcal infections, Canine herpes virus, Myxomatosis of rabbits, Paramyxovirus of pigeons and any other infective agent one wishes†. A regime of dosing over the first six months of life is usually required with perhaps, six monthly follow ups. Not only can these nosodes very effectively prevent the disease, without side effects or allergy, they can also greatly assist in the curing of the disease should it already have occurred. Professional advice on this subject should be sought since this form of homoeopathy must be considered as a type of vaccination. Your veterinary surgeon is best able to put these regimes into correct context of your home and your pet and he can also obtain new nosodes made up to suit your circumstances. As a general guide a preventive course of a nosode would consist of the following regime: A

---

* A much more consistent conventional vaccine has been produced since the 1st Edition, enabling a great percentage of pups to be vaccinated effectively at 12 weeks of age. This still does not, however, get around the difficult problem of vaccinosis (see Chapter 15)
† IJVH Vol 2, p. 45 Kennel cough (plus corrections in Vol 2 No 2, p. 57).

dose twice daily for a few days followed by monthly doses for up to six months of age, followed by six monthly boosters. These nosodes can also be used in the situation where a previous illness caused by one or other of these infectious agents has left a permanent mark on patient's health (see pages 36 and 113 and and Chapters 8/13).

Prevention of other foreseeable problems can be effected by the use of appropriate remedies. For example impending parturition: Caulophyllum, as has been seen in Chapters 8–13 has its sphere of action primarily in this field and can be used to extraordinary effect both in the treatment and prevention of parturient problems. Surgical shock or ill effects can be prevented by the use of Arnica, Calc. fl. or Staphysagria (see Chapters 8–13). Anaesthesia hangover can be prevented by the use of the appropriate remedy e.g. Chlorpromazine, Opium etc. Eclampsia can be prevented by the use of Calc. phos. Dental calculus can be lessened by regular dosing with Fragaria. All acute prescribing with homoeopathy is an attempt at 'preventive' medicine, since the correct remedy should forestall any tendency of the disease to go 'chronic'. It also in many cases prevents death or euthanasia or even surgery where conventional medicine is often unable to avert these dire consequences. Who can question the unrivalled power of Arnica and Aconite to prevent many of the ill effects of injury and associated shock. Blood loss into the tissue is lessened and as a result of this alone, further local tissue damage is prevented. Rickets and other disorders of bone growth can be prevented by Calc. carb., Calc. phos. and Mag. phos. Serious scarring after injury can be lessened or prevented by the use of Thuja and Silicea by mouth and Calendula topically. The use of Mercurial remedies in the treatment of eye ulcers can totally prevent further damage to the cornea. The ability to treat the unborn in utero (Eugenics) presents infinite possibilities for the prevention of disease since disease in the pregnant dam can create miasmic influences in the foetus. Emotional, dietary and infective conditions can influence the foetus seriously as can such problems as vaccinosis and other chronic diseases. (See also pp. 36, 83 and 135). The veterinary surgeon taking up homoeopathy will be delighted with the chance that this form of medicine gives him to control, mitigate or totally prevent many problems and conditions which hitherto had eluded his attempts at control, the items listed here being but an introduction to the world of homoeopathic preventive medicine.

Trial work to prove the efficency of nosodes in the prevention of Parvovirus, Distemper, Hepatitis, Leptospirosis or Feline Enteritis has not yet been performed (see Appendix 6 p. 181) Kennel Cough trials have, however, given dramatic results and much work has been reported on discases in farm animals and in catteries (influenza). These would seem to show that the nosode system is effective in principle but, until complete and fully controlled trials have been performed, owners must accept that the efficacy of these preventive remedies is unproven. Despite this cautionary remark, a great deal of anecdotal evidence has built up over the years and users of the nosodes report no problems and great confidence; their animals having withstood outbreaks of disease in their locality. The weight of this anecdotal evidence is overwhelming, and will, I am sure, be supported by statistical data in due course.

CHAPTER 15

The Relationship of Homoeopathy To Conventional Medicine and Diagnosis

It is often remarked that it is not possible to use Homoeopathic remedies either after conventional therapy or in conjunction with conventional therapy. As intimated in Chapter 2, I strongly believe that both these statements are false although the ideal may be valid. Firstly, I have successfully treated with homoeopathy a great many cases which have received conventional therapy immediately beforehand. Secondly, I do on rare occasions (as stated in Chapter 2) utilise conventional therapy to palliate disease in the terminally ill. Thirdly, when patients are already on conventional therapy they cannot always be abruptly taken off while Homoeopathy is commenced, the conventional drugs must often be 'tailed off'. Also there are those cases where one fails homoeopathically for one of many reasons (again see Chapter 2) and one cannot then deny the patient conventional therapy if there is a chance that it will do good. There is no room for dogma in medicine if one is not to be guilty of neglect of one's duties to patients (see Hahnemann's quote p. 9). Other therapies, too, can be brought in where considered helpful e.g. Acupuncture*, Anthroposophy, Bach Flower remedies, Biochemic Tissue Salts, Chiropractic, EAV, AK, Iridology, Radiaesthesia, Magnetic, Vibratory, Laser, Ultrasonic and Electrical ther-

*Acupuncture and homoeopathy should be compatible but I am suspicious that they may not be satisfactorily used simultaneously since they both attempt to shift energy patterns in the body. Their simultaneous use may invoke the problems associated with overprescribing (pp. 37/38, 46, 138) and consequently confuse or weaken the vital force, so I now use one or other alone at any one time until such time as more light can be thrown on this fascinating but elusive topic. Use of one at a palliative level and the other at deep level may be effective simultaneously (it is difficult to assess these things clinically). It is a fact that the Chinese support acupuncture with herbs (among other things) and homoeopathy may be able to fulfil this supportive role.

apies, Herbalism, Osteopathy, etc†. All may have a place from time to time and the byword of the ethical physician, whether human or veterinary, must be open mindedness. In more detail, then, under which circumstances might conventional therapy argue with Homoeopathy? Firstly in the case of Corticosteroid or, less emphatically, Antihistamine therapy it is believed there is a very real chance that homoeopathic treatment can be blocked. Prior to a homoeopathic remedy being prescribed on the Similia principle, in cases where such drugs have been used, one should use the potentised form of whatever agent has been used in order to speed its elimination from the system. Nux vomica, Sulphur and Thuja are also excellent remedies for 'clearing' the system of previous treatments. Long term corticosteroid therapy can sometimes be nearly impossible to clear, leading to total failure of natural therapy. Secondly, over-prescribing of drugs and over-long treatments can seriously 'muddle' the case, confuse the symptomatology and lower the 'vital force' of the patient. (Similar comments can be made about gross over-prescribing of homoeopathic remedies too, (see Chapter 6 pp. 37/38, 46, 137). Nux vomica, Sulphur and Thuja can all be used for 'Clearing' a case with a potentised form of the relevant drug.

There are, also, many cases where homoeopathy can actually undo the harm done by some conventional therapies. The harmful effects of radiotherapy and cytotoxic therapy can be helped by similimum prescribing. Vaccines may cause problems and here one would use Thuja as a first choice possibly followed by the appropriate nosode or potentised adjuvant. Over digitalised patients may be helped by Nitric Acid or Cinchona. Patients over treated herbally can be helped by Nux. vomica. Aloe has a reputation in helping those patients receiving too much antibiotic. The potentised forms of Corticosteroids, Hormones, Antibiotics and Anaesthetics can all be used in an attempt to reverse their respective ill effects. When more research is conducted many more such practices may well

† *I am certain that these therapies are complementary to each other. Where Homoeopathy fails another may prove useful. Radionics may possibly be subject to similar constraints as those postulated for Acupuncture in footnote★. The list of therapies has been expanded from the 1st Edition as a result of the Author's widening use of different therapies and cooperation with practitioners of such therapies.*

emerge as being beneficial. (pp. 36/37 and 139).

As stated in Chapter 2, adherence to veterinary homoeopathy does not mean the end of such commonsense practices as Fluid Therapy, Nutritional Therapy, Surgery, Nursing, Management and, for veterinary surgeons, correct communication with the pet owner. Nor does it mean the end of such necessary diagnostic procedures as Auscultation, Thermometry, Urinology, Haematology, X radiology, Bacteriology, Virology, Parasitology, Ophthalmoscopy, etc.; although these procedures are often over used at the expense of clinical observation and acumen. The homoeopath cannot hold himself above these things if he is properly to serve his patient. He may find himself relying for diagnosis on such tests less and less however (for it is true in general terms that modern methods rely on them too greatly, slowly losing respect for clinical instinct). Veterinary training can place too great an emphasis on 'science' and too little on the more important attributes of the real clinician, but there still must be a place for such tests and they should not be totally shunned*.

The modern homoeopath should set about reaping the benefit of the wealth of scientific lore which has accumulated since Hahnemann's day, putting it in its correct perspective, and combine all this with what he knows of the nature of disease, the nature of 'cure' (in the real meaning of the word) and the nature of medicine, gleaned from his study of Hahnemann's work and from his own open minded and philosophical approach to life. Surely, in doing so, he will establish that real ethic of veterinary medicine which can be directly lifted from Hahnemann's view of the physician's ethic so often quoted in this book (p. 9).

Vaccinosis: The varied problems arising from vaccination are worth discussing at this point. I have alluded to this problem elsewhere (p. 132, Glossary and IJVH Vol. 2 No. 1 p. 45 and Vol. 2 No. 2 p. 57 (corrections)). It is not a well documented fact that vaccination could be an erroneous strategy but evidence is building up, for those who wish to

---

On the matter of diagnosis itself the conventional diagnostic approach, with its intended end product of a specific name for any disease in question, is not such a relevant concept in Homoeopathy. I refer you to pp. 12, 16/17, 32, 103, 185 also to the Organon of Hahnemann, Paras 5–18 and 81 in which he expands upon this point very lucidly.

see, that all is not right with vaccination theory*. If such shreds of evidence (albeit often subjective) are not committed to paper for fear of ridicule then the problem will never be addressed by the scientific community and many valid observations from other vets will never see the light of day (for it is very often the case that observations which appear to fly in the face of current wisdom are misjudged by the observer and not recorded until such time as others record similar observations).

Occult vaccinosis describes disease arising remotely from vaccination. In individuals with a weak immune system it may conceivably be behind many cases of Eczema, Arthritis, Epilepsy, Allergy, Pancreatic insufficiency, immune deficient syndromes, feline gingivitis, miliary eczema and even Key Gaskell syndrome. Warts and Autoimmunity may also be predisposed by vaccination. Many cases of these conditions have appeared to improve with homoeopathic treatment only to relapse after booster vaccination, giving a clue to its possible involvement.

Overt vaccinosis: Blue eye in Afghan hounds with older poorly refined hepatitis vaccine, brain damage in humans following whooping cough vaccine, anaphyllaxis, frank illness following vaccination, lymphadenopathy, tonsillitis, etc. have all been witnessed as direct and obvious sequelae (albeit rare) to vaccination.†

I believe that it is beyond doubt that there is a problem. What is open to doubt, however, is just how big that problem is and this presents a huge open field for research. It is going to very difficult for anyone to acquire watertight proof of such a problem. What is important is that we must not discard the undoubted benefits of vaccination without a great deal of research into its effects, possibilities for refinement and possible alternatives.

---

* I am not alone in my fears with regard to Vaccinosis. Other authors have also referred to this problem and there are references to it, in Homoeopathic literature, going back a long way-even to Hahnemann, Organon, footnote to para 56.

† Irish Setters are particularly prone, in my opinion, to a tonsillitis following from vaccination, Haematological changes may also occur, Cavalier King Charles Spaniels may be similarly susceptive but more consistently react locally to the injection. I have no theory as to why there should be these particular breed susceptibilities but the pattern has emerged over the years.

Alternatives The nosodes present a very promising alternative for the protection of our animals against infectious disease. Work is being carried out on Distemper nosode and results of a trial on Kennel Cough (albeit on too small a scale) have been published (in IJVH Vol. 2, No. 1 p. 45 and additions Vol. 2, No. 2 p. 57). *The danger of airing a discussion such as this is that it runs the risk of creating anti-vaccination fear and prejudice of an unenlightened nature, leading to total lack of protection of animals against such killer diseases as Distemper, Parvovirus, Panleucopaenia, etc. This is clearly not my intention. The purpose of the discussion is to stimulate forward-looking and to throw light on possible lines of therapy for some of the chronic diseases mentioned.*

Treatment of vaccinosis: Such remedies as Pulsatilla, Lachesis, Silicea, Sulphur and Thuja are able to help the body get over the problem of vaccinosis. More specifically, the various nosodes and potentised adjuvants can be considered in an attempt to 'antidote' the effects of the particular fraction of the vaccine thought to be causing the problem. Do not forget the similimum or the constitutional remedy because this is arguably the only homoeopathic route to a complete cure.

CHAPTER 16

Selected Case Histories

These cases are chosen to demonstrate the method of selection of remedies and to give some indication of how the possible sequelae manifest themselves (see Chapter 6). Potencies are given here for the first time in the book. This section is not advising in this matter but merely reporting potencies used. The cases are grouped according to the level of prescribing chosen (see Chapter 5).

A) Treatment of the Root Cause/ Underlying Pathology

1 *An eighteen month old female cat admitted in emergency after a road traffic accident.* This cat was collapsed, breathing badly, pale and seemingly paraplegic. It appeared that the pelvis was broken and perhaps other injuries too but close examination would have been too distressing for the patient. The case appeared to be bad enough for euthanasia but the patient was given Arnica 30 at 15 minute intervals. By lunchtime the cat was making very good efforts to walk. 24 hours later an X ray showed a dislocated hip and multiple fractures of the pelvis. The patient was now quite strong enough for anaesthesia so the hip was replaced and cage rest over the next 3 weeks effected an apparent total recovery. Arnica 30 was given sporadically over the first three days.

2 *A two year old female cat brought in after a possible road traffic injury.* The cat was barely conscious, lying on its side and bringing up a lot of bright frothy blood from its lungs. Arnica 30 was administered every 5 minutes for half an hour then, since the cat brightened up enormously, only every two hours. The next day the patient was apparently normal. This was an unexpected outcome but can probably be explained by the fact that the haemorrhage was due to severe bruising of the lungs rather than gross tissue damage.

3 *A six year old male Jack Russell Terrier had been lame for almost a month in mid February.* The stifle joint in that leg had been found to be very loose, painful and noisy on movement. Rest had been advised for 3 weeks with stifle surgery at the end of that period if no improvement was observed, the pain was causing a great deal of depression in the patient and he was not able to move about much at all, even though the leg was always carried. Homoeopathic treatment was instituted in mid March. A mixture of Rhus tox., Ruta grav. and Arnica all in 30c potency was given twice daily for 10 days. Although the presenting symptom would have suited Bryonia better the possible pathology to muscles, ligaments, periosteum along with the resultant bruising and fear of being touched were all considered more important. Great improvement was noted after the 10 days not only in the ability to use the leg but in the personality and health of the patient and again after three weeks. After 1 month improvement had reached a plateau and Rhus, Ruta and Arnica in the 200c followed. Improvement again took place and surgery seems to have been averted.

4 *A four year old Chiahuahua female was brought in having previously had a stifle operation with prosthesis.* Ever since this the stifle had not been used properly and there had been a pink coloured discharge from the area periodically. It was decided to treat according to the pathology of a chronic suppuration rather than the historical line of treating for trauma to the joint. Silicea 30 was used three times daily for one month. Improvement was noted after two weeks and the discharge lessened. After several months the discharge was noted to be sporadic but the leg was back in use. Silicea has been used from time to time since and a constant but gradual improvement in the use of the leg has been noted throughout. The discharge has ceased.

B) Mental Level of Prescribing

1 *An eight year old male Golden Cocker Spaniel was showing successive signs of disease since February:* Itchy skin, epistaxis, pain at the hind end, and by October abject lethargy, overweight, skin troubles and showing no joy for life. He had been treated down the months conventionally and all but 'cured' of each of his symptoms. Thyroid treatment had come closest to producing a lasting effect. Homoeopathic treatment was started in December of that same year on the basis that in the previous December his lifelong companion, a 10 year old bitch Cocker had been put down, and that he was still, in the owner's opinion grieving. Ignatia 30c was used twice daily for just one week. After one month a distinct improvement in all aspects of his health was noted followed by a relapse, but to acceptable levels. The improvement in his sense of well being was especially reported. A further three day course of Ignatia 30c was prescribed. This again elicited a marked response to even better levels but again something of a relapse soon after. After two more episodes of improvement and relapse the owner reported a failure to obtain improvement overall. Ignatia 200 was prescribed one daily for three days, repeat as necessary. No more Ignatia has been required. An uneventful recovery has been reported. Most of all the owner is pleased to report the return of the patient's *'joie de vivre'*.

2 *A year old Golden Retriever bitch was involved in a car accident as an occupant of one of the cars.* This was on the way to the owner's office. Ever since that day (several months previously) the dog has dreaded going to the office and sat under the desk and shivered all day long. Leaving the dog at home all day was unacceptable so Homoeopathic treatment was sought. One dose of Aconite 1m was given followed by a week's course of Gelsemium 30c one daily. Here the historical aspects of the case were used as well as the presenting mental symptoms. An immediate improvement was reported and no further treatment has been necessary.

3 *An eight year old Collie cross male castrate was presented with chronic diarrhoea signs,* a quick and nervy nature, a stary coat and a fear of noises. No straining or pain was noted with the watery diarrhoea. Merc. sol. 30 was given twice daily for three days. The diarrhoea stopped but the nerviness became worse. The dog was afraid to leave the house. Since the chronic diarrhoea had stopped coincidental with the treatment, Merc. sol. 200 was chosen to get a deeper effect, despite the fact that the newly clarified mental symptoms did not quite fit. No result was obtained. Argent nit. 30c was then prescribed twice daily and an immediate improvement was noted. No further diarrhoea has occurred and the nerviness is no longer a problem. This demonstrates the need to return to first principles in prescribing.

4 *A six and a half year old Gordon Setter male was presented in November with epileptic fits which had started in May.* Clinically he was a nervy dog with a 'nervy' heart. Upon close questioning it was elicited that the fits usually occurred if one of the family was away. Ignatia 30 was prescribed twice daily for one week. Two months later no fits had occurred but the patient was biting his feet. He had always done this apparently before he ever showed epileptic fits although the history taking had not found this out. This was interpreted as a recapitulation phenomenon and Ignatia 200c was prescribed to be followed, if effective by 10M to achieve a deep and enduring effect. The condition resolved.

5 *A note of caution* would not be amiss at this juncture. A Cocker Spaniel came in very recently with very similar symptoms which started when the family moved house. The dog had been a rescue case and it was assumed the house move had brought about resurgence of the mental stresses undergone previously. Epileptic fits which were refractory to conventional therapy were occurring every 10 days. Ignatia 30 was prescribed but was followed by a severe aggravation. The dose rate chosen of one twice daily for four days was obviously too great and two days later the patient suddenly went down with nine fits in one day. This was stopped by heavy conventional therapy by a colleague and a cautious return to homoeopathy will be instituted soon, when it is certain that this effect has worn off. If fits become less frequent now it is certain Ignatia is the correct remedy.*

C) Treating at the Presenting Symptom Level

1 *An eight year old male neutered cat had received a bite on its right fore foot.* Infection had travelled up the leg to the elbow.

---

* *Since recording this case it was found that there followed a nine-week fit free period.*

The animal was very ill and running a temperature. There was much pain. Hepar sulph. 30c four times daily was prescribed and the report two days later was of a very fit cat with a slightly sore leg. All symptoms were gone at the end of the week.

2 *Near the end of May a 2 year old female Bulldog* came in by referral, the owner not wanting the bitch to undergo an ovarohysterectomy for the *pyometra* from which she was suffering. Polydypsia, Pyrexia, lymph nodes swollen and inappetance along with a pinkish purulent vaginal discharge served to confirm the diagnosis. Sabina 12c and Sepia 30 were given both twice daily. By the end of May the owner was happy that a complete recovery had occurred. Treatment was stopped. A check-up at the end of June confirmed the owner's opinion.

3 *A four year old neutered female cat was presented after months of eye treatment with a keratocoele on the right eye accompanied by vascularisation and pigmentation.* Merc. sol. 30c was prescribed since there was no photophobia and no apparent pain. Intermittent treatment with the remedy produced a marked but gradual response for two months, after which time only a tiny white mark on the cornea remained. The order of cure was firstly the keratocoele, secondly the pink colouration to that area, thirdly the vascularisation which receded towards the limbus and fourthly the pigmentation which appeared to peel off presumably as the cornea desquamated.

4 *A three year old Wolfhound bitch was referred with a congenital heart problem.* She displayed very poor exercise tolerance, cyanosis, dyspnoea and inappetance. She had been badly deteriorating for the previous three months but had never been really fit as a puppy. The heart sounds were rounded and diffuse and the rhythm was erratic with tachycardia. Digitalis 12x, Crataegus Ø, Viscum album 2x mixed tincture was given. A check one week later revealed that the tongue was properly pink, exercise tolerance was good, there was more crispness to the heart sounds but the rhythm had not returned to normal. Spartium 3c pillules and Convallaria Ø tincture were given, but a check after a week showed no further improvement in the heart or the patient. Spartium and Dig./Crat./Visc. were then adopted on

alternate days for one month then less frequently. The patient seemed to do very well and the heart sounds were good. She was not seen again until eight months later when she returned with rapid breathing, but she was still alert. Upon examination she was found to be suffering from constipation after eating a bone. Alumina 30c four times daily and increased frequency of Dig./Crat./Visc. tincture was prescribed to minimise the stress on the heart. Two days later all was well again. Six months after this a regime was adopted of one drop of Dig./Crat./Visc. tincture three times weekly with no Spartium. Six months later again she suffered from a brownish discharge after an abnormal normal 'heat'. She was grumpy which she had never been before. She was given Sepia 30c and responded in two days.

5 *An eighteen month old West Highland White bitch came in with Keratitis sicca (Dry Eye).* Four months previously the other eye had been affected, treated conventionally for one month and then been submitted for surgery (Parotid Duct transplant). This had ameliorated the condition but the initial damage to the cornea remained. When the second eye became affected it was Easter time and no referral for surgery was possible. Homoeopathic treatment and artificial tears were immediately instituted while surgery was being booked up. Zincum met. 30c twice daily was the treatment and artificial tears as necessary. It soon became obvious that artificial tears were needed less and less often until eventually the impending operation was cancelled and the artificial tears stopped. There was no damage to the eye and it is still completely healthy without treatment to date one year later.

6 *A three year old British Blue neutered male was brought in suffering from an intractible rodent ulcer* which had worsened despite conventional therapy for more than 6 months. The face was seriously disfigured. Con. mac. and Nitric acid were prescribed both in 30c. Within a week the paws broke out in lesions which discharged white creamy pus. His skin also broke out in lesions resembling miliary eczema. Both of these lesions had been displayed by this patient in the previous summer to his rodent ulcer. This was assumed to be a recapitulation process and therefore an indication of a correct remedy. However, after an initial improvement in the ulcer for one month no more improvement seemed to occur. The treatment was changed to Merc. sol. 30c along with Galium Ø tincture and Calendula lotion on the ulcer. Foot aggravation and skin aggravations again occurred. Nitric acid and Merc. sol. were used on different occasions for a period of one year and finally the lesion on the face has disappeared and the face remodelled so that it now appears normal. For the last six months of treatment one Merc. sol. 200 pillule per week or fortnight was prescribed depending upon response.

7 *A queen whose milk would not dry up* was given Cyclamen 30 by the owner since this had previously been successfully prescribed for a similar condition in another queen. Since no response was shown quickly a four times daily treatment was given for three days. The cat became ill, off her food, very slow and pyrexic. She was then brought in for veterinary attention and no mastitis or other disease could be found. The Cyclamen was stopped and the symptoms subsided almost immediately. This was a proving of some of the symptoms of Cyclamen which had been given too frequently and for too long and was the wrong remedy. Urtica 1x then dried up the milk.

8 *A kennel of Shelties suffered an outbreak of diarrhoea and vomiting.* The first puppy to contract the disease showed the symptoms of Merc. sol. (that is, wet mouth, thirst, yellow frothy vomit, painless diarrhoea, inappetance and smelly breath). It responded in a few hours. Successive members of the litter contracted similar symptoms were given the same remedy and responded except one. When the owner enquired about this non-response it was found that there was clear mucoid vomit and tenesmus with the diarrhoea. Merc. corr. was given and the response was rapid. This illustrates the need for close observation of symptoms and concomitants.

In a sensitive patient aggravations provings and recapitulations can occur very readily on what appear to be a very low dose of remedy. Each patient is different, and treatment 'according to results' is the only way to take this into account. Rigid appplication of dosage regimes without taking response into account can create difficult problems.

D) Treatment of Historical Problems

1 *A 9 year old Rottweiler male was referred with a history of upper respiratory problems.* There was noisy breathing, but no discharge, sneezing or other sign of disease. There was no history of tooth troubles and none could be found. The noisy breathing had started about 5 months previously. In the history-taking previous medical history revealed an operation to the right stifle coincidentally about five months previously. It was this historical event which was selected as the crucial point for prescribing since it was considered feasible that his palate or pharynx could have undergone bruising during or after anaesthesia. He was still lame on the stifle so the same pathology could have been instrumental in both symptoms. Rhus tox., Ruta grav. and Arnica (all in 30c) were prescribed and within two weeks the breathing was fine and the leg much better. A slight relapse after three weeks demanded a further short burst and now only the leg has occasional relapses.

2 *A working Collie was brought in because it had lost its sight.* The owner related it to a minor head injury about a year previously. He claimed that the vision had gradually been lost ever since that event so that now the Collie's useful life as a cow dog was finished at the age of two years. The eyes appeared to be normal by ophthalmoscopy but the dog was referred to a specialist anyway. No abnormalities were found. On the strength of the owner's conviction Arnica 200c was prescribed one pillule weekly. After one month the dog was back in work and to date has had no relapse.

E) Constitutional Prescribing

1 *A three year old Chiahuaha bitch had been exhibiting erratic hormone cycles.* When she was on heat it appeared thoroughly normal with normal bleeding. She had been mated three times but with no success. She was a timid creature with little thirst. Pulsatilla 30c was prescribed and a report eight months later stated that she had since brought up a litter of puppies.

2 *A seven year old Chiahuaha bitch was exhibiting a very dirty coat.* The coat was greasy, smelly and sparse. This condition had been continuing unabated for three years. The dog had a sad demeanour. Since the patient actually sought out somewhere warm to lie rather than be cool Psorinum 30c was chosen rather than Sulphur, within two weeks great improvement was seen in the coat and in the liveliness of the patient. After one month there was no more trouble.

These cases are not reported with the intention of 'proving' that homoeopathy works but rather as illustrations of the way in which it can be used. Many of the possible sequelae to treatment occurred in these few cases. Consistent reports from clients whose animals are on the correct remedy nearly always include a reference to the improved overall health and well-being of the patient, and very often include reference to the increased amount of sleep in the first twenty four hours. This latter finding may stem from a possible lack of rest in disease and the extra sleep being needed to catch up on rest.

CHAPTER 17

A Short Materia Medica of Some Key Substances

This chapter inevitably cannot contain all remedies or even a full coverage of the major ones, or it would be a book in itself. It is therefore confined to the main points of some major remedies and a few lesser ones in order to help in the use of the book (particularly Chapter 8). The bibliography (Appendix 5) will help in choosing further reading.

Aconitum napellus. One of the great fever remedies. Associated with fear nearly always, its symptoms are sudden in onset. Eyes are red and inflamed with watery discharge. There is usually photophobia. Ear pinna becomes red, hot and swollen. There may be nosebleeds of bright red blood usually with a sneeze. There may be signs of soreness of the throat. Vomiting with thirst is seen and a painful abdomen. Urine is usually red and hot. There is a hoarse cough with Aconite, tachycardia, full bounding pulse.

Symptoms are usually brought on by or aggravated by cold, dry winds.

Actaea racemosa. (Cimicifuga) With its affinity for the musculoskeletal system, nervous system and female sexual systems it is used mostly in these contexts.

Restlessness of the limbs, stiffness and spasm in neck and back regions. Chorea and jerking, pain in lumbar and sacral regions are all seen. Ovarian and uterine symptoms are often associated with the locomotor problems.

Symptoms are usually worse in the morning and better for warmth.

Allium cepa. Frequently turned to in cases of coryza where there is watery discharge, bland from the eyes but acrid from the nose. There is often photophobia. There can be a hoarse cough, and symptoms are usually worse in the evening, or in a warm room and better for open air or cold room.

Aloe socotrina. The diarrhoea symptoms often govern the choice of this remedy. There is distended abdomen, the stool may be passed involuntarily with much flatus. The stools are often mucoid and the anus sore. The remedy is also useful to re-establish health after long, heavily treated illness where symptoms are confused.

Alumina. Debilitated old patients showing weak muscles and constipation characterise the remedy's main prescribing points. Mucous membranes and skin tend to be dry and inflamed. One can therefore see conjunctivitis, otitis externa and dry hard stools passed with much straining. Sometimes there is absence of desire to pass the stool because of the paretic state. Nails are often brittle. Symptoms are worse in the morning and in a warm room, better for open air and in the evening.

Ammonium Carbonicum. Indicated where there is wheezing, laboured respiration typically in overweight patients with a weak heart and probably showing a harsh cough. The nose may be stopped up at night and there may also be nosebleeds.

There may also be urinary incontinence at night. Symptoms are worse in evenings and in the middle of the night. Worse for wet and cold, better for dry weather.

Antimonium Tartaricum. Is characterised by a loose rattling, unproductive cough, such as is often heard in cats. Respiration can be very difficult with much gasping. There is usually thirst for little and often. Symptoms are worse in the evening, lying down, and in cold damp weather or warm room.

Apis mellifica. This remedy is of great use in conditions characterised by shiny oedematous swellings which 'pit' on pressure. There is usually a great desire for open air particularly if there is respiratory involvement. (eg pulmonary oedema). Apis is suited to conjunctivitis with chemosis where the conjunctiva 'bubbles' out, acute or chronic pulmonary oedema, swollen shiny joints and also in cases of nephritis with urine retention. It has a diuretic action too. It is particularly of use in cases of vulval injury where oedema can prevent urination. Symptoms are worse for heat or touch, better for open air and cold bathing.

Argentum Nitricum. Purulent ophthalmia with abundant discharge, corneal ulceration, corneal opacity are all symptoms of this remedy. Trembling nervousness, particularly if it leads to stomach disorders or diarrhoea, also responds well.

Symptoms are worse for warmth and at night, better for fresh air and cold.

Arnica montana. This is homoeopathy's great *injury* remedy and should be used in all cases of injury and surgical interference, especially dental extraction. Bruising and ecchymoses characterise its symptoms, also fear of being touched. It is often forgotten that it has powerful antiseptic properties too. It can be used internally or as a lotion or ointment. It is of use to help symptoms of over-exertion.

Arsenicum Album. Anxiety or restlessness are often present where this remedy is indicated. Discharges from eyes or nose are watery and acrid causing ulceration in those regions. The mouth is usually dry and the patient is usually thirsty. Dramatic vomiting and diarrhoea, often simultaneously, indicate its use if concomitant signs agree. The patient may have wheezing respiration, and allergic asthmatic conditions can respond well. The skin can be dry, scaly and scruffy. Skin and respiratory signs alternate. An important constitutional remedy.

Symptoms are worse for cold and wet, better for warmth.

Belladonna. This is one of the great fever remedies, conditions requiring its use usually being of *violent* and sudden onset. Heat, redness, pain and swelling characterise its symptoms. It is one of many remedies of use in convulsions. Pupils are usually dilated so its use in *Key-Gaskell Syndrome* in *cats* is well known but it is only one of many in this condition also. Acute ear inflammations where there is heat, pain and swelling respond well. The mouth is usually dry and there is a great thirst.

Symptoms are worse for noise, touch or jarring motion and better for quiet, dark, rest and slight warmth.

Bellis perennis. As with Arnica it is useful for injury but more especially deep muscular bruising or pelvic injury. Think of it therefore post partum, for instance, and after deep orthopaedic surgery. Where there is stumbling and weakness in late pregnancy it is also indicated.

Bryonia alba. This remedy shows both diarrhoea and constipation symptoms, the latter usually in chronic conditions. The mouth is often dry and there is a great thirst. The tongue is often coated yellow. It is of great help in many cases of rheumatism or arthritis where symptoms agree. There are often respiratory signs with a hoarse, hacking cough. Mastitis will respond if modalities are correct. All symptoms are *markedly worse for movement* and better for rest, (p. 94).

Calcarea Carbonica. A constitutional remedy of major importance classically in overweight, slightly sluggish patients usually displaying skeletal disorders or delayed dentition. Eye symptoms include pupil dilation, blocked lachrymal ducts or even cataract. Chronic catarrh can occur. There is usually an increased appetite which may be depraved. Lymph nodes in the throat are often enlarged and there may, in addition to bone growth abnormalities in the young, be umbilical herniation. The skin has an unhealthy appearance and a tendency to warts. Symptoms are usually worse for exertion, cold and water; better for dry weather.

Calcarea Fluorica. Is especially useful where hard swellings feature among the symptoms. Glandular swellings and mammary growths are an example. Bony malnutrition of puppies can be helped and it has a reputation for helping control adhesions after abdominal surgery. Symptoms are worse for rest and damp, better for exercise and warmth.

Calcarea Phosphorica. This remedy is similar in action to Calcarea Carbonica but suits better the leaner patient. Bony puppies, appearing out of proportion, showing a depraved appetite, delayed dentition, epiphyseal malformation and arthritic changes resulting from this all indicate this remedy. Patients are often more active than Calc. Carb. Symptoms are worse for cold and damp, and better for warm dry conditions, (p. 94).

Calcarea Sulphurica. Slow healing, discharging, purulent lesions respond well to this remedy. Discharges are usually yellow. It can help chronic catarrh, cystic growths and thick, yellow discharges. In contrast to Silicea it is most effective when discharges have found an outlet.

Calendula officinalis. Is chiefly used topically, as a lotion or ointment, applied to wounds and abrasions. It promotes rapid healing and controls sepsis, having a great value on open wounds and ulcers.

Cantharis vesicatora. This is an irritant poison with a predilection for the urogenital system and skin. Hence homoeopathically used classically in cases of cystitis where straining is a feature with blood in the urine. Urine is usually passed in tiny amounts very frequently, some unproductive efforts also being made. Skin lesions are vesicular rashes. Burns and scalds respond to this remedy.
   Symptoms are worse for touch, better for rubbing.

Caulophyllum. This remedy is primarily used in all conditions *relating to parturition*; before, during and after. It controls and aids preparturient relaxation of the tissues, uterine contractions, expulsions of the foetus, expulsion of the foetal membranes and, finally, involution of the womb. This is if it is given as a prophylactic measure. When this has not been done, it is still of great use at any stage and can even help to clear up post parturient metritis. This remedy is also associated with pains in the small joints especially if these are during or after pregnancy. (p. 94) (See also Veterinary Record, and see p. 181).

Causticum A remedy whose prime action is on the neuromuscular system* and skin. Warts which are rough, and flat respond well. Rheumatism better for warmth and generalised stiffness call for Causticum. Chronic cystitis and intertrigo also may respond. Symptoms are worse in cold dry conditions, better in warm damp conditions. A constitutional remedy. (p. 94).

Chamomilla. Primarily known for its action *on teething* problems it can bring relief to a great many health problems arising at the nursing stage and after in young animals. Conditions which arise at this time may be skin problems,

----

* Paretic tendency

epilepsy, diarrhoea, colic, swelling of the lymph nodes and abdominal tympany. In nearly all cases there are signs of an irritable response to pain or interference. Nursing problems in the mother (e.g. painful mammae) and even false pregnancy may respond.

Chelidonium majus. A liver remedy of major importance its symptoms are those of obstructive jaundice, congested liver, diarrhoea alternating with colic – stool yellow or clay coloured depending upon whether there is obstruction of the bile system or not.

Symptoms are usually worse for movement and touch and early mornings, better after food.

Cinchona officinalis. This is Hahnemann's historic *Peruvian bark*. Periodic fevers, sweats, cold skin and great debility are the main sphere for Cinchona. The pulse is usually thready and weak, haemorrhages when present are usually dark clots. There is sensitivity to touch. Should always be considered in dehydrated patients after illness.

Symptoms are usually worse for touch, draughts and after food, better for warmth and open air.

Cistus canadensis. Hard glandular swellings typify this remedy, especially those of throat and neck and the mammae. The mouth is usually cold and smelly with swollen gums. When growths ulcerate and when the patient feels the cold badly, Cistus could be of help. Ears often show a watery purulent discharge.

Cocculus. Inability to open the mouth or swallow with drooling and vomiting in some cases indicate Cocculus. It acts on the central nervous system and is therefore an epileptic remedy. Symptoms are always worse for prolonged movement so it is one of the *travel sickness* remedies.

Coffea cruda. Acts upon the nervous system to produce restlessness, agitation and sleeplessness particularly in the small hours. Hypersensitivity of skin, intolerance of pain and discomfort after food with a bloated abdomen are classical Coffea symptoms.

Symptoms are worse for noise and better for warmth.

Colchicum autumnale. With Colchicum there is coldness and prostration and usually a gassy distended abdomen.

The patient is unwilling to allow legs to be stretched out. There is thirst and cravings but offerings of food are then refused. This often fits the picture of the hunting cat with a gassy tummy, inappetance, inactivity and coldness. It is also of use in some forms of arthritis, usually when joints are red, hot and swollen. Symptoms invariably worse for movement. (p. 94).

Colocynthis. A remedy for *spasmodic colic* where, as with Colchicum but more markedly, the legs are hunched up compressing the abdomen. There may be a tight distension of the abdomen and is usually a flatulent diarrhoea which produces temporary relief. There is usually much mental agitation. The patient often grinds teeth and is worse for noise. Hip pain may respond.

Conium maculatum. The remedy is characterised by weakness and trembling particularly in the aged, and particularly starting at the hind limbs. Ageing symptoms of the eyes and limbs especially can be helped as are many tumours especially those of the lymph glands and mammae. Chronic ulceration may also be associated. With eye symptoms pain is uppermost. It is the first choice remedy for CDRM in German Shepherd dogs and similar symptoms in other breeds. Symptoms are worse when lying down or rising and from exertion but are better for motion.

Crataegus. Is a heart tonic remedy helping irregularities of rhythm, weakness from chronic heart disease, oedema of dependent parts or generalised oedema (dropsy). Dyspnoea on least exertion, dilated heart, weak heart sounds and valvular murmurs.

Digitalis. As with Crataegus this is a heart remedy, for use when pulse is weak, irregular and slow, but quickened by least effort, heart is weak and dilated, when dropsy occurs and when there is a tendency to fibrillation. The tongue may become blue and the patient may even be helped when actual heart failure has occurred.

Drosera. Coughing with retching or vomiting is a good indication for this remedy. Spasmodic dry coughing attacks following closely upon each other with changes in the voice are characteristic. It appears as if something were caught in the throat. Symptoms are worse lying down, warmth after midnight and for swallowing or excitement.

Euphrasia. Is mainly of use in conjunctivitis where there is photophobia, catarrhal corrosive discharge, sticky mucus on cornea, and frequent blinking. Symptoms are worse for warm winds, evening, light and better in darkness. Use in the form of eye drops as well as internally.

Gelsemium sempervirens. Mentally this remedy is useful for anticipatory fear, show fright, fear of thunder, some forms of epilepsy and in excitable male dogs. Fear and nervousness can lead to urination and can root the patient to the spot. There is usually some weakness and trembling in the limbs. It has been used successfully to treat nystagmus following cat flu.

Symptoms are worse for damp, impending storm, excitement, better for open air and continued activity.

Graphites. A constitutional remedy, it is indicated in the smelly skinned dog which enjoys the fireside. The skin is usually dry and itchy, hair falls out, and ears and eyes have a watery purulent discharge. The skin in the folds of the limbs may crack and discharge. Symptoms are worse for warmth and at night.

Hamamelis virginica. Extravasation of blood, ecchymoses, passive venous haemorrhage which fails to clot (dark, seeping haemorrhage) weakness from loss of blood and pain in large open wounds or postoperative pain can all be greatly helped by Hamamelis. Aids resorption of blood clots.

Hepar Sulphuris. Is a major remedy for use in cases of *suppuration*. Typically lesions are very sensitive to touch. It should be used to prevent suppuration when specific injury has occurred (e.g. cat bite) and should also be used if signs have developed. It also aids resorption of pus (e.g. hypopion) and cures or prevents cellulitis. Symptoms are worse for touch and cold, better for warmth.

Hypericum perforatum. Reduces pain in open lacerated wounds and in closed injuries where tissues are rich in nerve endings (e.g. toes, tail). Post operative pain and spinal injury may be greatly helped and it should be used, along with Ledum, to *prevent tetanus* developing from puncture wounds.

Symptoms are worse for cold and touch.

Ignatia. Should always be considered where there is evidence of insecurity or agitation arising from abandonment, *bereavement* or loneliness. This can be triggered by loss of a human or fellow-animal companion. Hysteria, self mutilation, skin disease, epilepsy and general fading can all result from the above emotions and close history taking can often reveal their involvement. It has also been successfully used in weaning problems of mother and offspring.

Ipecacuanha. Vomiting repeatedly, associated with respiratory embarrassment call for this remedy. Attacks can lead to collapse. Nose bleed of bright red blood and similar haemorrhages from the womb, blood in the milk of suckling mothers and post operative vomiting are all good indications for its use. Symptoms are worse as lying down and show a periodicity.

Kali Bichromicum. Is characterised by *yellow ropy* discharges. It acts mainly upon the membranes of the eyes, gastro intestinal tract and respiratory system. The eyes show swelling of the lids, the characteristic discharge and even corneal ulceration. Pain is not usually prominent. Chronic catarrh again shows characteristic discharge and rawness of nares and obstructed nose. If there is a cough it is productive again with characteristic expectoration. Urine is similarly affected. Vomiting will usually produce bright yellow water and the stools are brown and frothy. Symptoms are worse in the morning and in hot weather but better from local heat.

Kali Carbonicum. Great weakness and intolerance of cold weather with irritability and hypersensitivity are properties of this remedy. Sac-like swellings appear in upper eyelids and eyelids stick together in the morning, nose becomes blocked in a warm room. Nasal discharge is yellow and thick, but not viscid, nostrils are made sore and ulcerate. In the female weakness and debility after parturition is seen, in the male weakness after coition. A wheezing cough with or without hydrothorax can be seen. Symptoms are worse for cold weather, and in the small hours; better for warm weather and for movement.

Kali Chloricum. Essentially its action lies in destructive kidney disorders. Chronic nephritis with putrid breath, acrid saliva, ulcerated mouth. If there is diarrhoea it is greenish. Urine albumen and phosphates are high and there is often blood.

Ledum palustre. Think of this remedy in conjunction with puncture wounds (also Hypericum). It has a strong *antitetanus* reputation and also aids wound healing. Symptoms are worse at night and for heat, better for cold.

Lillium tigrinum. One of the great female remedies. Patient is usually depressed and fidgety. Congestion of pelvic organs with offensive bloody discharge from the womb while moving, ceases when still. There is often an urgent desire to defaecate. There is often an increased thirst. One of the remedies useful in Pyometra in bitches. (p. 82).

Lycopodium clavatum. Exerts most of its effect on the digestive organs, liver, kidneys and respiratory system. The patient dislikes being left alone and appears apprehensive. The nose is often blocked and there may be blisters on the tongue. Eating a little food always satisfies appetite but appetite is very marked. The belly is usually bloated. The stool appears small and hard and is expelled only with difficulty accompanied by ineffectual straining. Urination is also a slow process and urine has a red sediment. There is often an irritating cough. Symptoms are worse for heat generally and better for cold. A constitutional remedy.

Mercurius Corrosivus. Aptly named, this constitutional remedy acts on corrosive destructive processes. The ears discharge greenish pus. The eyes show acrid tears often with corneal ulceration and intense photophobia. The eyelids are reddened with excoriation. Mouth ulcers appear and the breath is foul with profuse, acrid saliva. The alimentary system is similarly affected, great thirst being present with much vomiting of clear mucoid fluid. Diarrhoea is painful producing much tenesmus. The kidneys undergo similar corrosive changes leading to haematuria and albuminuria. There is also tenesmus on urinating. Purulent wet eczema often responds to this remedy. Symptoms are worse evening and night, better resting.

Mercurius Solubilis. Is a very similar remedy to the above, but showing less dramatic symptoms. There is usually no photophobia, chronic vascularised eye ulcers respond well, vomit is usually yellow and there is no tenesmus with the diarrhoea. High potency suppresses suppuration.

Natrum Carbonicum. Is a thunder remedy. It can be of help in heat exhaustion, milk-induced diarrhoeas, chronic catarrh, especially if odorous, and patients subject to easy spraining of joints.

Symptoms are worse for summer heat, thunder storms, draughts. Better for movement.

Natrum Sulphuricum. Should be remembered in cases of *head injury*, possibly resulting in brain damage. Also in cases of meningitis. There is usually photophobia. Abdomen is flatulent and diarrhoea (especially in the morning) is involuntarily passed with flatus.

Symptoms are worse for damp weather, better for dry weather.

Nitric Acid. A notable wart remedy (for those which bleed easily) it also acts strongly on mucocutaneous junctions. Lesions which are around this region respond well (e.g. rodent ulcer). Any lesion which bleeds freely should lead one to consider this remedy.

Symptoms are worse for hot weather and night time.

Nux vomica. Primarily used in the digestive sphere its greatest reputation is in helping disturbances following overeating of *unsuitable foods*. Faeces is usually hard but diarrhoea can follow overeating. There is abdominal discomfort, flatulence, irritability and sensitivity to noise. It is also used in cases of umbilical herniation in young animals. It is one of Homoeopathy's 'clearing' remedies, and a great constitutional remedy.

Symptoms are generally worse for noise and better after rest or for damp weather.

Petroleum. This remedy is very useful in preventing *travel sickness*. Skin symptoms which also call for it are dryness, cracks, redness, rawness, easy bleeding. There can also be dry lesions around eyes and ears.

Symptoms are worse in damp weather and from travelling, better for warm air and dry weather.

Phosphoric Acid. One of several remedies of use in debility, especially if diarrhoea is present. There is usually apathy, dehydration and loss of condition. There can be an association with grieving. Diarrhoea is usually yellow and of a painless nature. It can help regulate bone growth. Symptoms are worse for exertion, better when warm.

Phosphorus. Is a very 'sudden' remedy. The patient is sensitive to loud and sudden noise (eg thunder storms, fireworks etc.). Degenerative processes and bone destruction respond to Phosphorus. Food is suddenly vomited back when it has been warmed in the stomach, gums can be ulcerated and bloody. Hepatitis, jaundice, pancreatic disease and nephritis come into its sphere. Urine may be bloody. A very painful cough is also a symptom affecting the whole body. Wounds which perpetually bleed can be helped. The patient is usually in poor body condition. An important constitutional remedy.

Symptoms are worse for touch, exertion, evening and during thunder storms; better for cold and sleep.

Phytolacca. Glandular swellings are its greatest field of action usually associated with debility and restlessness. Lymph nodes and mammary gland swellings are red, hard and sensitive. Throat involvement is common with difficult swallowing and red discolouration. There are also shifting rheumatic symptoms and a tendency to boils.

Symptoms are worse for exposure to damp, cold weather, motion and at night, better for warmth, dryness and rest.

Picric Acid. Neurasthenia, notably in oversexed male dogs, characterises this remedy. Also weakness associated with prostate problems in old dogs. Young dogs can reach a state of near paralysis with foaming mouth. Extruded penis is also a sign.

Symptoms are worse for exertion and in wet or hot weather; better for cold.

Platina Metallicum. Is one of the predominantly female remedies. An aloof-seeming patient usually over-hungry with irregular and abnormal hormone cycles is typical. Usually the abnormality tends to nymphomania rather than lack of sexual behaviour. (See p. 81).

Podophyllum. Is primarily a diarrhoea remedy. It is characterised by colicky pain, sometimes vomiting of bile and gushing offensive stool which contains mucus and is usually painless. There is often a greenish colour to the watery faeces. There can also be a concomitant prolapsing of the rectum.

Symptoms are worse in early morning and in hot weather.

Psorinum. Besides Sulphur this is the best known mange remedy. It is the nosode of the human scabies vesicle. Its symptoms are a smelly dirty skin and coat, scurfiness and chilliness in a patient which craves heat.

Symptoms are worse for changing weather, cold and hot sunshine; better for warmth.

Pulsatilla nigricans. One of homoeopathy's great female remedies, suiting best the patient of shy, yielding disposition. Disorders of the female hormone system respond well when the type fits. Discharges whether from nose, eyes, vulva, etc. are creamy. Another pattern which responds well is that of symptoms which *come and go*, e.g. appetite, diarrhoea, itchy eyes. There is usually little thirst. The patient is cheerful but easily dispirited. A common constitutional type. (See p. 81).

Symptoms are worse for heat, towards evening; better open air, motion, cool.

Pyrogenium. Is valuable in toxaemic febrile conditions especially where there is a weak pulse. Think of it in puerperal fevers and where discharges are putrid. Think also of Echinacea in this connection.

Rhus toxicodendron. Is the most famous of the *rheumatic* remedies. The skin and musculoskeletal system are its main spheres. Small red papules in the skin, and sometimes vesicles, are typical lesions with much scratching. Cellulitis may occur. In all cases of damage to muscles think of Rhus and the symptoms of Arthritis/Rheumatism which respond are those which are worse after rest particularly if this follows strenuous exertion. The symptoms improve with limbering up, only worsening on excessive exertion. Classically the worst pains are seen as the animal rises from its bed. (p. 93).

Ruta graveolens. Is a powerful remedy in cases of sprain or dislocation. If there is any damage to fibrous structures such as tendons, ligaments or periosteum turn to Ruta. Symptoms as with Rhus are worse after rest.

Sabadilla. Is a help for sneezing coryza with red sore eyes. The throat can be affected, causing frequent swallowing movements. The patient is sensitive to cold. Symptoms are worse for cold and better for warmth.

Sabal serrulata. Has its greatest reputation in the treatment of prostatic disease. Loss of sexual power and general evidence of irritability of the urogenital system indicates its use. In the female, underdeveloped mammae may be helped.

Sanicula. Is indicated when discharges have an offensive fishy odour. It has proved of use in recurring anal gland problems where this has been used as a pointer. Painful constipation, where desire only occurs after great quantities accumulate, expelled with great difficulty, often recedes and crumbles. Fishy vaginal discharges also. Travel sickness cases can also be helped, in patients displaying a fear of downward motion.

Sarsaparilla. Is primarily a urinary remedy being particularly effective in cases of urethral obstruction. Sabulous plugs or calculi can both respond. There is usually tenesmus, pain and blood.

Sepia. A famous 'female' constitutional remedy notable for its effect on the 'darker' mental side of female hormonal aberration. False pregnancy bitches with unpredictable bad temper typify it. Pelvic organs are usually slack with a tendency to prolapse. Membranes may be slightly yellowed and the patient is sensitive to cold. (See p. 81).
Symptoms are worse for cold air and before a thunder storm; better for exercise, warmth and after sleep.

Silicea. Fits the shy, chilly patient who is reluctant to enter the consulting room. Chronic inflammatory conditions such as sinuses and granulomata respond well. If the cause be a *foreign body* then so much stronger the indication. It is surprising how often a foreign body such as a grass seed, splinter, thistle or thorn (or even bone fragment from an injury) can create a low grade inflammatory response which fails to eject it. If abscessation and discharge occur then the lesions frequently heal and open again and again. Use Silicea and be prepared for a long term treatment (as long as three weeks in some cases).

Spongia. The coughing patient with little exercise tolerance, congested lungs and resting for long periods in sternal recumbency is a good subject for Spongia. The cough is usually better after eating.

Staphysagria. This remedy is associated with the mental state of resentment which is difficult to define in animals. It is also of use in post-operative complaints and in problems in maiden bitches after their first mating.

Stramonium. This is a convulsion remedy primarily. Some cases of epilepsy respond. Pupils are dilated. Prefers light to dark. Graceful rhythmic rather than jerky choreic movements of limbs.

Symptoms are worse alone, in the dark. Better in company in the light.

Sulphur. This is the most famous mange remedy. Constitutionally the typical patient is dry, dirty coated, smelly, overweight and stubborn. It dislikes heat and chooses if possible to lie on a cold floor. The skin is typically red over the whole patient. Mucocutaneous junctions are nearly invariably reddened. Difficult respiration can occur with a desire for open air. If concomitant symptoms agree both diarhoea and constipation can respond. This remedy is one of the homoeopath's weapons for 'clearing' the system of overtreatment or poisoning.

Symptoms are worse for heat and at rest.

Symphytum. Its common name is 'knitbone' and this is its main action – promoting effective healing of fractures. It should be used in all such cases (along with Arnica) to ensure adequate callus formation and optimum resolution. It is effective in combating the effects of peri orbital, orbital and eye injury (Sclera) too.

Thuja occidentalis. A *wart remedy* of primary importance when warts are pedunculated. Anal adenomata may respond. When adverse reaction to vaccination has occurred

Thuja can offer almost immediate relief in many cases. A constitutional remedy.

Urtica urens. Urticarial reaction in the skin responds well to Urtica, where there is acute irritation, small red weals and great agitation. Burns and scalds respond well (see Cantharis). Low potency suppresses milk in engorged mammae and high potency stimulates it. Agalactia responds well to the treatment. Urinary suppression also indicates this remedy. Symptoms are not helped by cold water (cf. Apis) in fact the opposite is the case.

Veratrum album. Cases of dysentery where the patient is cold, cyanotic and collapsed indicate this remedy. The pulse is usually rapid and weak and the coldness very marked. The remedy helps to control dehydration.

Viscum album. Lowered blood pressure with a slow pulse, respiratory difficulty, hypertrophic heart with valvular incompetence. Useful in the treatment of some cancers. Symptoms worse in winter and for movement and the patient prefers sternal recumbency.

Zincum Metallicum. A convulsion remedy where, in between fits, there is great depression. The patient is sensitive to noise but lethargic. The eyes roll and there can be conjunctivitis especially the inner canthus. 'Dry Eye' can respond to this treatment. Colic occurs after eating.
Symptoms are worse for touch and after food.

Glossary of terms met in this book and in Homoeopathic Literature in general

ACUTE DISEASE: Is one which is of rapid onset and short duration. It implies nothing of its severity. The outcome is death or recovery.

ADJUVANT: Material added to a conventional killed vaccine to enhance local reaction with the intention of bettering resulting immunity.

AGGRAVATION: Worsening of symptoms associated with the administration of a correct remedy at an incorrect potency.

ALLOPATHY: System of medicine utilising agents to treat disease which are totally unrelated to the disease in their action.

ANTIBIOTIC: An antimicrobial therapeutic agent originally synthesised by living organisms (e.g. Fungi). Now many are artificially synthesised.

ANTIOPATHY: System of medicine utilising agents to treat disease which are opposite to the disease in their action.

BLEPHAROSPASM: Spasm of the eyelids.

C: See Centesimal

CENTISIMAL: Scale of dilution of a remedy each stage being one in one hundred.

CHEMOTHERAPEUTIC: A chemical agent used in conventional medicine to combat bacterial or protozoal infection e.g. Antibiotic, Sulphadimidine.

CHRONIC DISEASE: Is one which is of long standing and well established, there is no period of resolution.

CONCOMITANT SYMPTOM: Is one which accompanies the presenting symptom and is a useful aid to prescribing homoeopathically.

CONSTITUTIONAL REMEDY: Is one which takes the entire make up of the patient into account, rather than presenting symptoms and concomitants alone. The nature of the

	body's programmed response to disease.
CORTICOSTEROID:	A steroidal agent produced by the Adrenal Cortex or a synthesised analogue of this. Anti-inflammatory and highly suppressive in action (Steroid qv). Also called Cortisone.
CURE:	The total elimination of disease and restoration of health.
d:	See Decimal.
DECIMAL:	Scale of dilution of a remedy each stage being one in ten.
DISEASE:	Dynamic disturbance of the harmony existing between the 'Vital Force' in a body and the material body itself. Literally Dis-Ease.
ENDEMIC:	A disease (usually transmissible) which exists among a certain human population and usually reaches a balance with that population.
ENZOOTIC:	As above but applies to animals.
EPIDEMIC:	A disease (usually transmissible) which is not in balance with a human population and is spreading.
EPIZOOTIC:	As above but applies to animals.
EPISTAXIS:	Nose bleed.
EUGENICS:	The treatment of the unborn in utero as an attempt to eliminate disease acquired in utero as a result of maternal ill-health or miasmic influence.
EUTHANASIA:	Humane killing of patient usually to avert suffering from terminal illness.
GENERALS:	Symptoms applying to the whole body.
HETEROPATHY:	See Allopathy.
HOMOEOPATHY:	Treatment of disease with a substance which has the power to reproduce symptoms similar to those displayed.
HYPER–:	Prefix denoting excess.
HYPO–:	Prefix denoting insufficiency.
IMMUNITY:	Is the ability to resist infection usually by means of circulating or tissue antibodies.
INTUSSUSCEPTION:	Telescoping of the bowel.
ISOPATHY:	Treatment of disease by the identical agent of the disease. Here vaccination has similarities. (See also NOSODE).
LESION:	Change produced by disease in tissue or organ.
MATERIA MEDICA:	Book of provings of remedies

MIASM:	Hahnemannian term for infective agent. No direct definition in modern medical terms exists.
MODALITY:	Modification of symptoms by such influences as temperature, time, motion, weather etc.
MOTHER TINCTURE:	Undiluted alcoholic solution obtained from original plant material. The starting point for all potencies from soluble material. (Denoted by Ø)
NEOPLASIA:	Literally 'New Growth'. Usually reserved for cancer (also malignancy).
NOSODE:	Homoeopathic remedies prepared from infected tissue, disease discharges or causal organisms (see Isopathy).
NYSTAGMUS:	Rhythmic, jerky movements of eyes usually laterally, usually involuntary.
OPISTHOTONUS:	Describes the posture of an animal in extensor spasm, that is, head and neck back, legs outstretched, back arched.
OVAROHYSTERECTOMY:	Surgical removal of ovaries and womb
PALLIATIVE:	Treatment aimed at directly reducing symptoms (antiopathy).
PARENTERAL ROUTE:	Is a route of administration of a medicine other than via the alimentary canal (e.g. Injection).
PARTICULARS:	Symptoms applying to individual organs, organ systems or parts of the body.
PATHOLOGY:	The science which deals with the cause of and changes produced by disease – usually confined to demonstrable tissue changes.
PHOTOPHOBIA:	Literally 'fear of light'. Describes the blinking of animals when confronted with light to which they are over sensitive.
PLACEBO:	Medicine given to humour, rather than cure, the patient. A psychologically induced cure may follow – 'the Placebo Effect'.
POLYCREST:	One of the deep acting consistently applicable remedies which have a wide action on all parts of the body. Constitutional remedies are polycrests.
POTENCY:	The dynamic principle of a remedy harnessed in the dilution/succussion process. Quantified by c or x (d) and number of stages undergone.
POTENTISATION:	The above process. (Trituration qv)

PROSTHESIS: Surgical insertion of foreign material to correct anatomical deficiency or injury.

PROVING: The administration of a remedy to a body sufficient to cause symptoms noted in the materia medica. A poor translation of the German, Prüfung – a test.

PYREXIA: Fever.

RECAPITULATION: The recurrence of past elements of a chronic disease (often seemingly unrelated to present symptoms) as a result of homoeopathic treatment. These past elements are usually symptoms suppressed by Antiopathy.

REGULATORY REMEDY: One which has opposite action at high and low potencies.

REPERTORY: Book of symptoms with indicated remedies.

SIMILIMUM: A remedy closely matching the symptoms exhibited by the patient, the ideal homoeopathic remedy.

STEROID: Sterol-related substances having a basic chemical configuration based on Cyclopetenophenanthrene which is an unsaturated hydrocarbon. Synthetic analogues also exist. (see also Corticosteroid)

SUCCUSSION: The agitation process applied to homoeopathic remedies at each stage of dilution during the potentisation process.

SUPPORTIVE THERAPY: Arguably part of nursing rather than medicine. Applies to fluid and nutritional supplementation given to a weak patient. Blood transfusions, artifical lungs, oxygen therapy, renal dialysis, etc.

SYMPTOM: Homoeopaths view is that a symptom is the result of the patient's fight against the disease. The discernible properties of the disease process in the patient by which one decides upon a remedy.

TENESMUS: Straining e.g. at faeces or urine.

THERAPEUTIC: Remedial.

TRITURATION: Dilution of insoluble material with milk sugar prior to subsequent liquid dilution as per potentisation (qv).

VACCINATION: Administration of live attenuated or killed disease agent to protect a patient against that or similar specific disease (see also Isopathy).

VACCINOSIS: Disease resulting from vaccination

VITAMIN: Derived from 'Vital Amine'. Essential ingredients of diet playing a part in cellular chemistry, structure of tissues, function of nerves, integrity of membranes and immune responses. Supplementation can be an essential part of medicine.

X: See Decimal.

Remedy List

There follows a list of the Common names of remedies (where these differ from the Latin names) with their Latin equivalents and Common abbreviations.

Common Name	Latin Name	Abbreviation
Aconite	Aconitum napellus	Acon.
Acrid Lettuce	Lactuca virosa	Lact. v.
Aloe	Aloe socotrina	Aloe.
Aluminium Oxide	Alumina	Alum.
American Arum	Caladium seguinum	Calad.
Ammonium Carbonate	Ammonium carbonicum	Ammon. carb.
Ant	Formica	Form.
Apomorphine	Apomorphia	Apomorph.
Arbor Vitae	Thuja occidentalis	Thuja.
Argilla	Alumina	Alum.
Arsenic Trioxide	Arsenicum album	Arsen. alb.
Atropine	Atropinum	Atrop.
Balsam Apple	Momordica balsamina	Momord.
Baneberry	Actaea spicata	Actaea sp.
Barberry	Berberis vulgaris	Berb.
Bichromate of Potash	Kali bichromicum	Kali. bich.
Bitter Cucumber	Colocynthis	Coloc.
Black Lead	Graphites	Graph.
Black Snakeroot	Cimicifuga (Actaea racemosa)	Cimic. rac.
Blood Root	Sanguinaria	Sanguin.
Bluebell	Agraphis nutans	Agraph.
Blue Cohosh	Caulophyllum	Cauloph.
Blue Flag	Iris versicolor	Iris.
Borate of Sodium	Borax	Borax.
Bounafa	Ferula glauca	Ferula.
Bromide of Potash	Kali bromatum	Kali. br.
Bryony	Bryonia alba	Bryon.
Bugle Weed	Lycopus virginicus	Lycopus.
Buttercup	Ranunculus bulbosus	Ran. b.
Bushmaster (see Surucucu)	Lachesis	Lach.
Calabar Bean	Physostigma	Physost.
Calcium Carbonate	Calcarea carbonica	Calc. carb.
Camphor	Camphora	Camph.
Carbonate of Barium	Baryta carbonica	Baryta carb.
Carbonate of Lime (see Calcium Carbonate)		

Carbonate of Potash	Kali carbonicum	Kali. carb.
Caroba Tree	Jacaranda	Jacar.
Cat Thyme	Teucrium marum	Teuc. mar.
Cayenne Pepper	Capsicum	Caps.
Cereus (see Night Blooming)		
Cevadilla Seed	Sabadilla	Sabad.
Chamomile	Chamomilla	Cham.
Chaste Tree	Agnus castus	Agn.
Cherry Laurel	Laurocerasus	Lauroc.
Chick Pea	Lathyrus sativus	Lathyr.
Chlorate of Potassium	Kali chloratum	Kali. chlor.
Christmas Rose	Helleborus niger	Helleb.
Club Moss	Lycopodium	Lycop.
Cobalt	Cobaltum	Cob.
Cobra	Naja tripudians	Naja.
Cockroach	Blatta americana	Blatta.
Coffee	Coffea	Coff.
Comfrey	Symphytum	Symph.
Condor Plant	Condurango	Condur.
Copper	Cuprum metallicum	Cupr. met.
Coral Snake	Elaps corallinus	Elaps.
Corn Smut	Ustilago maydis	Ustil.
Corrosive Sublimate	Mercurius corrosivus	Merc. cor.
Cotton	Gossypium	Gossyp.
Cowhage	Dolichos puriens	Dolich.
Crawfish	Astacus fluvatilis	Astac.
Creosote	Kreosotum	Kreos.
Croton Oil Seed	Croton tiglium	Croton tig.
Cuban Spider	Tarentula cubensis	Tarent. cub.
Culvers Root	Leptandra	Lept.
Cuttlefish Ink	Sepia	Sep.
Cyanide of Mercury	Mercurius cyanatus	Merc. cyan.
Daisy	Bellis perennis	Bell. per.
Damiana	Turnera	Turn.
Deadly Nightshade	Belladonna (Atropa)	Bell.
Duck Weed	Lemna minor	Lemna.
Dusty Miller	Cineraria	Ciner.
Elder	Sambucus niger	Samb.
Ergot	Secale cornutum	Secale.
Eyebright	Euphrasia	Euphr.
Flea	Pulex irritans	Pulex.
Flint	Silicea (or Silica)	Sil.
Fluorspar	Calcarea fluorica	Calc. fluor.
Fool's Parsley	Aethusia cynapium	Aeth.
Fowler's Solution	Kali arsenicum	Kali. ars.
Foxglove	Digitalis purpurea	Digit.
Fringe Tree	Chionanthus	Chion.

Galipea cusparia bark	Angustera vera	Angust.
Glauber's Salt	Natrum sulphuricum	Nat. sulph.
Goa	Chrysarobinum	Chrysarob.
Goat's Rue	Galega officinalis	Galega.
Gold	Aurum metallicum	Aurum.
Golden Ragwort	Senecio aureus	Senec.
Golden Seal	Hydrastis	Hydr.
Goose Grass	Galium aparine	Galium ap.
Gravel Root (see Queen of the Meadow)		
Greater Celandine	Chelidonium majus	Chel.
Ground Holly	Chimaphila umbellata	Chimaph.
Gypsum	Calcarea sulphurica	Calc. sulph.
Hawthorn	Crataegus	Crat.
Hedge Hyssop	Gratiola	Grat.
Hemlock	Conium maculatum	Con. mac.
Henbane	Hyoscyamus	Hyosc.
High Cranberry	Viburnum opulis	Viburn. op.
Honey Bee	Apis mellifica	Apis mell.
Horse Chestnut	Aesculus hippocastanum	Aesc. h.
Hydrochloric Acid (see Muriatic Acid)		
Hydrofluoric Acid	Fluoricum acidium	Fluor. ac.
Indian Cockle	Cocculus	Cocc.
Indian Hemp	Apocynum cannabinum	Apoc.
Indian Tobacco	Lobelia inflata	Lob.
Indigo	Baptisia tinctoria	Bapt.
Iodide of Arsenic	Arsenicum iodatum	Arsen. iod.
Iodide of Lime	Calcarea iodata	Calc. iod.
Iodide of Potassium	Kali hydriodicum	Kali. hydriod.
Iodine	Iodum	Iod.
Ipecac Root	Ipecacuanha	Ipecac.
Iron	Ferrum metallicum	Ferr. met.
Jaborandi	Pilocarpus microphyllus	Piloc.
Jack in the pulpit	Arum triphyllum	Arum triph.
Jambol Seed	Syzigium	Syzig.
Jelly Fish	Medusa	Med.
Jequirity	Arbrus precatorius	Arbrus.
Jerusalem Oak	Chenopodium anthelminticum	Chenop.
Knitbone (see Comfrey)		
Kombe Seed	Strophanthus	Stroph.
Lead	Plumbum metallicum	Plumb. met.
Leopard's Bane	Arnica montana	Arn.
Lily of the Valley	Convallaria	Convall.
Lucerne	Alfalfa	Alf.
Lungwort	Sticta pulmonaria	Sticta.

Male Fern	Filix mas	Filix. m.
Mandrake (see May Apple)		
Mare's Tail (See Scouring Rush)		
Marigold	Calendula officinalis	Calend.
Marjoram	Origanum	Orig.
Marking Nut	Anacardium orientale	Anac.
Marsh Tea	Ledum palustre	Ledum
Meadow Saffron	Colchicum autumnale	Colch.
Mercuric Sulphide	Cinnabaris	Cinnab.
Mercury (see Quicksilver)		
Mistletoe	Viscum album	Viscum.
Monkshood (see Aconite)		
Night Blooming Cereus	Cactus grandiflorus	Cactus
Nitroglycerine	Glonoinium	Glon.
Nutmeg	Nux moschata	Nux. m.
Onion (see Red Onion)		
Orange Spider	Theridion	Ther.
Pasque Flower	Pulsatilla nigricans	Puls.
Passion Flower	Passiflora	Pass.
Pennywort	Hydrocotyle	Hydrocot.
Peruvian Bark	Cinchona officinalis	China or Cinch.
Pheasant's Eye	Adonis vernalis	Adon.
Phosphate of Iron	Ferrum phosphoricum	Ferrum phos.
Phosphate of Lime	Calcarea phosphorica	Calc. phos.
Phosphate of Magnesia	Magnesia phosphorica	Mag. phos.
Phosphate of Potassium	Kali phosphoricum	Kali. phos.
Picrate of Iron	Ferrum picricum	Ferrum Pic.
Pine Tar	Pix Liquida	Pix liq.
Pink Root	Spigelia	Spig.
Pipsissewa (see Ground Holly)		
Plaster of Paris (see Gypsum)		
Poison Ivy	Rhus toxicodendron	Rhus tox.
Poison nut	Nux vomica	Nux vom.
Poison Weed	Wyethia	Wyeth.
Poke Root	Phytolacca	Phyt.
Pomegranate	Granatum	Gran.
Poppy latex	Opium	Opium.
	(Papaver somniferum)	
Potash Alum	Alumen	–
Potassium Hydrate	Causticum	Caust.
Primrose	Primula obconica	Prim. obc.
Prussic Acid	Hydrocyanic acid	Hydrocyan. ac.
Puffball	Bovista	Bov.
Purple cone Flower	Echinacea (Rudbeckia)	Echin.
Purple Fish	Murex	Mur.

Quebrachio	Aspidosperma	Aspid.
Queen of the Meadow	Eupatorium purpureum	Eup. purp.
Quicksilver	Hydrargyrum	Hydrarg.
	Mercurius solubilis	Merc. sol.
Quinine Sulphate	Chininum sulphuricum	Chin. sulph.
Radish	Raphanus	Raph.
Ragwort (see Golden Ragwort)		
Rattlesnake	Crotalus horridus	Crotal. horr.
Rattlesnake Bean	Cedron	–
Red Onion	Allium cepa	All. cep.
Red Starfish	Asterias rubens	Aster.
Rock Rose	Cistus canadensis	Cistus
Rudbeckia (see Purple Cone Flower)		
Rue	Ruta graveolens	Ruta grav.
Saffron	Crocus sativa	Crocus
Sage	Salvia officinalis	Salvia
Sal Volatile	Ammonium carbonicum	Ammon. carb.
Salt	Natrum muriaticum	Nat. mur.
Savine	Sabina	Sab.
Saw Palmetto	Sabal serrulata	Sabal serr.
Scabies Nosode	Psorinum	Psor.
Scouring Rush	Equisetum	Equiset.
Shepherd's Purse	Thlaspi bursa	Thlaspi.
Silico Fluoride of Calcium	Lapis albus	Lapis alb.
Silver Nitrate	Argentum nitricum	Argent nit.
Skullcap	Scutellaria	Scut.
Smilax	Sarsaparilla	Sarsap.
Snakewort	Senega	–
Snow Rose	Rhododendron	Rhod.
(Helleborus is also sometimes referred to as Snow Rose)		
Sodium Biborate	Borax	Bor.
Southern Wood	Abrotanum	Abrot.
Sowbread	Cyclamen	Cycl.
Spanish Fly	Cantharis	Canth.
Spanish Spider	Tarentula hispania	Tarent hisp.
Sponge	Spongia	Spong.
Spurge Olive	Mezereum (Daphne)	Mez.
St Ignatius Bean	Ignatia	Ign.
St John's Wort	Hypericum	Hyper.
St Mary's Thistle	Carduus marianus	Carduus mar.
Starfish	Asterias	Aster.
Stargrass	Aletris farinosa	Aletr.
Star of Bethlehem	Ornithogallum	Ornith.
Stavesacre	Staphisagria (Staphysagria)	Staphis. (Staphys.)
Stinging Nettle	Urtica Urens	Urt.
Stone Root	Collinsonia canadensis	Collins.
Sulphate of Lime	Calcarea sulphurica	Calc sulph.

Sulphate of Potassium	Kali sulphuricum	Kali sulph.
Sulphide of Antimony	Antimonium crudum	Ant. crud.
Sundew	Drosera	Dros.
Surucucu (Bushmaster)	Lachesis	Lach.
Tartar Emetic	Antimonium tartaricum	Ant. tart.
Thornapple	(Datura) Stramonium	Stram.
Thoroughwort	Eupatorium perfoliatum	Eup. perf.
Tiger lily	Lilium tigrinum	Lil. tig.
Tin	Stannum metallicum	Stan. met.
Toadstool	Agaricus	Agar.
Tobacco	Tabacum	Tabac.
Ucuba	Myristica sebifera	Myr. seb.
Valerian	Valeriana	Val.
Vegetable Charcoal	Carbo. vegetabilis	Carbo. veg.
Verdigris	Cuprum aceticum	Cupr. ac.
Virgin's Bower	Clematis erecta	Clem.
Virgin Vine	Pareira brava	Par.
Water Hemlock	Cicuta virosa	Cic.
White Bryony (see Bryony)		
White Hellebore	Veratrum album	Verat. alb.
Wild Cherry	Prunus virginiana	Prunus v.
Wild Indigo (sec Indigo)		
Wild Liquorice (see Smilax)		
Wild Strawberry	Fragaria	Frag.
Witch Hazel	Hamamelis	Ham.
Woody Nightshade	(Solanum) Dulcamara	Dulc.
Wormseed	Cina	–
Yarrow	Millefolium	Millef.
Yellow Dock	Rumex crispus	Rumex.
Yellow Jasmine	Gelsemium	Gels.

Common Potency Levels

United Kingdom

Decimal potencies are rarely used but these are the potencies in which they commonly appear in the UK:

1x, 3x, 6x, (12x) these are low potencies.

Centesimal potencies are much more common. The customary potencies available are:

3c, 6c, 12c, 30c, 200c, M and 10M
3c is low. 6c and 12c are transitional. 30c and 200c are high.

M and 10M refer to dilutions of 1/100, one thousand times and 1/100 ten thousand times respectively. These are very high potencies and more rarely used in veterinary work.

6c is the commonly obtainable potency.

If no suffix letter appears then assume c, that is Sulphur 6 is in fact Sulphur 6c.

Mother tincture is denoted by the Greek letter Ø (see p. 169). Several remedies will appear in the text, recommended as mother tinctures.

Trituration: (see p. 170) is used for insoluble material.

Europe

European countries use different potencies from the United Kingdom, as their commonly prescribed remedies.

Firstly, instead of x suffix they use d prefix to denote decimal potencies. So 6x will appear as d6.

Secondly their common potency levels are:

c4   c5   c7   c9   c15   c30 etc

alternatively:–

4 c.H.   5 c.H.   7 c.H.   9 c.H.   15 c.H.   30 c.H. etc.
(cH = centesimal Hahnemannienne)

This can contribute to confusion when meeting European remedies on holiday, where homoeopathic remedies are more widely obtainable than in the United Kingdom, or should you have such remedies in the cupboard from previous imports.

Other systems: You may find LM potencies mentioned, or Korsakoff potencies. These are beyond the scope of this small book.

Useful Addresses

Blackie Foundation
101 Harley Street, London W1N 1DF.

British Homoeopathic Association
27a Devonshire Street, London W1N 1RJ. 071 935 2163.

British Homoeopathy Research Group
Secretary, 101 Harley Street, London W1N 1DF.

British Veterinary Association
7 Mansfield Street, London W1M 0AT. 071 636 6541.

British Small Animal Veterinary Association
5 St George's Terrace, Cheltenham, Glos. GL50 3PT.

British Association of Homoeopathic Veterinary Surgeons
Secretary, Chinham House, Stanford-in-the-Vale, Nr Faringdon
Oxon SN7 8NQ. 0367 710324

Hahnemann Society
Hahnemann House, 2 Powys Place, Great Ormond Street,
London WC1N 3HT.

Faculty of Homoeopathy
Royal London Homoeopathic Hospital, Great Ormond Street, London
WC1N 3HR. 071 837 8833.

Homoeopathic Trust
Hahnemann House, 2 Powys Place, Great Ormond Street, London
WC1N 3HT. 071 837 9469.

National Association of Homoeopathic Groups
Secretary, 11 Wingle Tye Road, Burgess Hill, West Sussex RH15 9HR.

International Association for Veterinary Homoeopathy
President and UK representative, Chinham House, Stanford-in-the-
Vale, Nr Faringdon, Oxon SN7 8NQ.

Royal London Homoeopathic Hospital, Great Ormond Street, London
WC1N 3HR 071 837 8833.

Bibliography

* A Veterinary Materia Medica — George Macleod, MRCVS, DVSM.
* Homoeopathic First Aid Treatment For Pets — Francis Hunter, MRCVS.
* Guide to the Homoeopathic Treatment of Beef and Dairy Cattle — Christopher Day, MRCVS.
* Homoeopathic Medicine for Dogs (Translation) — H. G. Wolff.
Homoeopathy First Aid in Accidents and Ailments — D. M. Gibson.
* Homoeopathy for Pets — George Macleod, MRCVS, DVSM.
* Natural Health for Dogs and Cats — Pitcairn and Pitcairn.
Materia Medica with Repertory — Boericke.
† Organon of Medicine 5th and 6th Edition — Hahnemann, Dudgeon and Boericke.
† Organon of Medicine (New translation) — Hahnemann, Künzli, Naude and Pendleton.
Repertory of the Homoeopathic Materia Medica with Word Index — Kent.
* Dogs: Homoeopathic Remedies — George Macleod, MRCVS, DVSM.
* Veterinary Toxicology (Garner's) — Clarke and Clarke.
* The Treatment of Cattle by Homoeopathy — George Macleod, MRCVS, DVSM.
* The Treatment of Horses by Homeopathy — George Macleod, MRCVS, DVSM.
Homoeopathic Drug Fixtures — M. L. Tyler
† Introduction to Homoeopathic Medicine — H. Boyd
† The Handbook of Homoeopathy — G. Koehler
* Cats: Homeopathic Remedies — George Macleod, MRCVS, DVSM.

JOURNALS: (See Appendix 6)

COURSES (See p. 25)

† Useful books on the principles of Homoeopathy
* Purely veterinary books

The others are of great use and relevance. Although purely human in text, much can be adapted for veterinary use.

Research

This is a brief outline of some the heartening research that is going on into the mechanisms and effect of homoeopathy.

1 Study of the homoeopathic potentised solutions to try to discover what principle is involved in their make-up. Why is a 'potentised' solution different from a simple diluted solution of the same concentration? Such work includes studies of the crystallisation properties of the solutions, viscosity studies, studies of the molecular structure of the solvent etc.

2 Clinical trials in doctor's surgeries and veterinary surgeries to determine the efficacy of remedies against specific diagnosed syndromes in individual cases. Such studies include work on Hay Fever, Rheumatism, Travel Sickness etc.

3 Clinical trials in intensive farm situations to determine the efficacy of specific remedies in controlling specific problems e.g. Dystocia, Mastitis, Milk Fever etc. See Veterinary Record 1984 Vol 114 pp 216.

4 Clinical trials in boarding kennels and rescue kennels to ascertain the efficiency of the nosodes in the protection of dogs against the great epizootic diseases to which they are prone e.g. Kennel Cough IJVH Vol 2 No 1 p. 45 with addendum in Vol 2 No 2 pp. 57), Distemper (paper to be published) etc.

5 Provings on healthy human volunteers using potentised remedies. These studies are consistently providing evidence that remedies, in potency, can produce an effect. Few have been done on animals.

Such journals as the 'British Homoeopathic Journal', 'Homoeopathy Today', 'Homoeopathy', 'The Veterinary Record' and 'The Journal of The British Homoeopathic Research Group' serve to publish the results of British work in these fields. The International Journal for Veterinary Homoeopathy, founded in 1986, collects papers from all over the world on the subject of veterinary homoeopathy and research.

It is only by continuing these efforts that the required proof of the efficacy of the Homoeopathic method will be obtained and a better understanding of its mechanisms. When these objectives are realised much more will be learnt about how to use homoeopathy because it will be an accepted, widely used and widely discussed form of medicine with a healthy exchange of ideas bringing new lines of thought to everyone's notice. Roll on that day!

Uses of Homoeopathy in Conventional Veterinary Medicine

It is interesting to note that the benefits of the homoeopathic mechanism are being exploited unwittingly by orthodox medicine in a great variety of ways, showing that with a small change in approach there are common areas between homoeopathy and conventional medicine. This is heartening for the future of medicine since it makes it all the more likely that an open mind to homoeopathy can be adopted. A few examples here will serve to illustrate the claim:

Digitalis: Toxic symptoms include prolonged systolic period and fibrillation.

Uses for Digitalis in conventional therapy include shortening systole and controlling fibrillation. This is a case of similia similibus curentur.

Sulphur: Many skin dressings contain sulphur to cure skin diseases. Symptoms of toxicity of sulphur, when applied topically, include skin irritation.

Arsenic: Arsenical compounds are used less frequently now than they used to be of late as an effective control of Swine Dysentery. Acute Arsenic toxicity includes vomiting, watery diarrhoea often with blood, exhaustion, collapse and death. Chronic poisoning produces wasting and unthriftiness with a weak and irregular pulse. These are the symptoms of Swine Dysentery in acute and chronic form.

Copper: It is now widely accepted that copper bracelets (collars for dogs) can help some rheumatism/arthritis cases. It is arguable that those cases which do respond are the homoeopathically indicated patients which would respond to copper in potency. (There may also be electrical field effects).

Gold: Similar arguments could be applied for those patients who respond to gold injections.

Fluorine: This applies only to human medicine. Fluorine is administered to the United Kingdom population in the drinking water to prevent the symptoms of dental decay. Fluorine poisoning would produce exactly those symptoms!

Quinine: Derivatives are still used to combat Malaria and this was the substance which Hahnemann 'proved' in his first studies in 1790 as capable of producing Malaria type symptoms.

Nux vomica: Is still used in Stomach Powders for cattle. It is used as a digestive aid and colic treatment. An upset digestion and abdominal pain are among the symptoms of Nux vomica poisoning.

Ipecacuanha: There is still a conventional proprietary compound cough remedy available which contains Ipecacuanha – a potent cough-producing substance!

Acute Disease, Chronic Disease and the Miasms

It is beyond the scope of this book to go deeply into theories of Acute and Chronic disease and Hahnemann's Miasm theory but it is salutory to focus one's mind on the problem even if only for a short while. Besides one cannot read deeply into homoeopathic literature without coming across references to the Miasm theory of chronic disease. This discussion is put in the appendix since it is of philosophical and academic interest, rather than essential to the study of homoeopathy.

ACUTE DISEASE is of rapid onset and short duration and if the attack on the body is not too severe the basically healthy body will eventually throw off the disease and recover. If the onslaught is too severe then death will result.

CHRONIC DISEASE is one of long standing. The patient and the disease reach a type of equilibrium. There is no period of resolution.

Both words are sometimes erroneously used to imply a level of *severity* of disease. This is not implied in either word.

Hahnemann taught that one should, in the treatment of disease:

1 Select a homoeopathic remedy, that is, one which has the power to reproduce similar symptoms in a healthy body.

2 Try to resist suppressive antiopathic treatment; this may produce in the case of chronic disease deeper, more difficult symptoms; and in the case of acute disease can convert it into a chronic disease.

3 Allow the remedy time to work. A chronic disease is deep seated and will not disappear immediately. Often, the order of cure follows the pattern:

a) From within outwards (in the case of skin disease this can often involve a worsening of the skin condition before a cure is obtained).
b) From centre to extremities.
c) Newer symptoms disappear before older ones.

The Miasm Theory

Hahnemann believed that all chronic human diseases stemmed from three basic (infective) 'miasms': Psora (the itch), Sycosis (Gonorrhoea) and Syphylis. He believed that the many variations seen in chronic disease arise from the continued passage of these infections through countless generations of humans and countless distinct individual constitutions subjected to a great number of extrinsic factors. Suppression of the symptoms he believed led to a driving inward of the chronic disease so that it could express itself as Cancer, Asthma, Paralysis, Nervous Debility or Epilepsy (he cited many more examples). He believed that there is a dormant seat of one or other or any combination of the three miasms in most individuals and that this might flare up at any time as a result of stress to the system eg puberty, marriage, childbirth, bereavement etc. Each of life's stresses can contribute to a break down of one's inherent resistance to the dominant miasm.

Hahnemann firmly believed that it was folly to study cellular processes and other detailed disease symptoms but that one should simply choose for treatment, a homoeopathic remedy selected according to the similia principle. He said in a similar vein, that it was folly to present the many and varied manifestations of chronic disease as diseases in themselves under a multitude of particular names or to try to adapt a certain general medicine to any of them.

A deeper study of his thoughts on this subject can be found in the Organon, see Appendix 5.

Whether or not one can accept Hahnemann's archaic and definite views on chronic disease is open to question but if there is anything in what he said then modern views of chronic disease must change. His lack of modern scientific knowledge and his pedantic prose make his theories seem fanciful but one must resist the temptation to dismiss them out of hand. Modern medicine still falls into the trap of imposing certain general names on diseases as well as adapting certain general medicines to them. Those who intend to take up homoeopathy must, in order to derive the most benefit from the method, change their way of thinking from the latter and concentrate more on learning about a disease from its totality of symptoms rather than its name. Always bear this in mind when using Chapter 8 et seq. for guidance in choosing a remedy, the required remedy for a particular case may not be listed, and without this approach failure (always a possibility owing to our human frailty) is much more certain (see p. 45).

Veterinary Surgeon's List of First Remedies Incorporating Home Starter List

Once having taken up the challenge of homoeopathy it is essential to have on hand a number of useful remedies for contingency purposes. I have made a list which I can recommend as being the ones most likely to be useful under most domestic circumstances. They also constitute a very useful list for the veterinary surgeon taking the first plunge. Without a handy list like this there is very little to guide one's choice from the several thousand remedies available.

Internal Medicines
* ★ Aconitum napellus
* ★ Apis mellifica
* Argentum nitricum
* ★ Arnica montana
* ★ Arsenicum album
* Belladonna
* ★ Bryonia alba
* Cantharis
* Caulophyllum
* Chamomilla
* Colocynthis
* Gelsemium
* ★ Hepar. sulph.
* Ledum
* ★ Mercurius corrosivus
* ★ Mercurius solubilis
* Petroleum
* Pulsatilla
* ★ Rhus toxicodendron
* ★ Ruta
* Sanicula
* Sepia
* Silicea
* Symphytum
* ★ Urtica

Lotions or creams
* ★ Arnica
* ★ Calendula
* Euphrasia Eye Lotion
* Hamamelis
* ★ Hypericum

The particular uses of these remedies are given in Chapters 8–14 and one should refer to these chapters and further reading for a reasonable understanding of their need to go on an 'essentials' list. Some of the circumstances for using these remedies demand veterinary involvement to ensure that no medical trouble can ensue from failure to pick up important symptoms. For example an apparent cystitis in a cat, leading one to use Cantharis perhaps, could in fact be a case of urolithiasis in which the urethra is blocked and urination is obstructed. Veterinary examination will reveal this, owner treatment may not and delay could be fatal. Other remedies can be a useful adjunct to conventional veterinary methods, for example, Arnica and Symphytum in the case of a fractured leg. Arnica will reduce the tissue damage and bleeding and the resultant pain, Symphytum will hasten healing. Be assured that no harm can follow from the use of these remedies. There are no side effects but some repercussions can occur which can be mistaken for side effects†.

The common potencies obtainable are listed and explained in the Appendix section. The potencies used in this country are, by convention, different from those used in Europe and some of these are listed too.

* *Signifies the remedies most useful in home starter kit for animals.*
† *The one exception to the rule is the case of Silicea which has the power to reawaken an old encapsulated lesion of tuberculosis. This is a very unlikely eventuality in this day and age. See also Provings p. 46, Recapitulation p. 44 and Aggravation p. 45.*

Homoeopathy in Tortoises, Snakes, Lizards and Fish

Poikilotherms are those animals which do not maintain their own body temperature but are totally at the mercy of the external environmental temperature. They are commonly called 'cold-blooded' but that is a relative term. Their body temperature can be very high but only when the surroundings are very warm or when they bask in the sun.

Species commonly encountered in veterinary work are **Tortoises** (which hibernate) and their relatives, **Snakes**, **Lizards** and **Fish**. Homoeopathic work with these creatures is mainly confined to local or pathological prescribing (according to the same principles discussed for other species) as and when individual illnesses arise but an attempt can be made to aim for constitutional remedies in certain cases. I am always reminded, when discussing these creatures, of the **Monitor Lizard** (a 'small' carnivorous iguana) which was constipated, off food and malevolently angry. He was also highly reactive to noise and disturbance. This was Nux vomica if ever I saw it and a single injection of Nux sorted the problem very rapidly! Cleo the **Reticulated Python** was presented to me 'vomiting' blood and lethargic. She was also periodically thrashing with obvious abdominal discomfort. She had lost interest in her surroundings. She had last been fed two week earlier. It transpired that her environment was too cool (the species is indigenous to tropical rain forest) and I assumed she was suffering chilling with her food not being digested properly, resulting in some putrefaction. I gave Phosphorus 30c by injection, according to 'constitutional' prescription, and Pyrogenium in low potency. Cleo had started to recover by the next evening. A **Tortoise** was brought in suffering from respiratory problems. She was off food and had a right sided conjunctivitis. Lycopodium was the treatment of choice and a good outcome ensued. Lycopodium appears to suit the tortoise appearance very well, as too can Causticum Hahnemannii. Eggbound tortoises will respond very well to Caulophyllum usually within twenty four hours. The fish which I have treated have been treated more according to 'herd' principles, which I have discussed in my book on Cattle medicine, but individuals may also be treated. I have not knowingly prescribed 'constitutionally' for these creatures as I have established no feel for fish constitutional manifestations. Treatment has been by nosodes or by local/pathological methods only. This differs in no way from mammalian medicine when practised on the same principles but 'in water' treatment takes on a new meaning!

In general terms speed of response to remedies seems, in practice, to be governed more by life-style and general reactivity than body temperature. Horses and cats react very quickly to life's stimuli and so too to homoeopathic treatment. Tortoises react slowly, the Monitor Lizard reacted very quickly both in life-style and medically. Do not be afraid to apply homoeopathic principles to these 'exotic' species, just because they are unusual visitors to the veterinary surgery. They are able to respond according to identical principles to those learnt for dogs and cats.

Index